# LOVE
# SWEETER
# LOVE

*Sweet Simplicity Series*

# LOVE SWEETER LOVE

## Creating Relationships of Simplicity and Spirit

by
Jann Mitchell

BEYOND
WORDS
Publishing
I   N   C

Beyond Words Publishing, Inc.
20827 N.W. Cornell Road, Suite 500
Hillsboro, Oregon 97124-9808
503-531-8700
1-800-284-9673

*Editor*: Ann Bennett
*Design*: Connie Lightner
*Illustrations*: Lydia Hess
*Typesetting*: William H. Brunson Typography Services
*Proofreader*: Marvin Moore

Printed in the United States of America
Distributed to the book trade by Publishers Group West

*Library of Congress Cataloging-in-Publication Data*

Mitchell, Jann.
  Love sweeter love : creating relationships of simplicity and spirit / Jann Mitchell.
    p.  cm.—(Sweet simplicity ; v. 2)
  Includes bibliographical references (p.   ).
  ISBN 1-885223-73-0
  1. Man-woman relationships.  2. Marriage.  I. Title.  II. Series.
HQ801.M578  1998
306.7—dc21                                                      97-49137
                                                                    CIP

For Ted.
who has shown me the
many facets of love.
What a ride!

# CONTENTS

# FOREWORD

I love reading Jann Mitchell's books. They're fun, solid, honest, real, and wise. And this is, of course, true of *Love Sweeter Love*. This encyclopedia of simple truths about love teaches us much about creating and maintaining beautiful relationships, not only with others, but with ourselves.

You will find in these pages the truths about real love, rather than romantic love—which usually isn't love at all; it's need. I always maintain that if Romeo and Juliet, our model of "the greatest love story ever told," had hung out with each other for another six months, they would surely have broken up! Needy people can't sustain real love. Another fairy tale bites the dust!

Jann and I wholeheartedly agree that the most important truth about loving ourselves and others is that we must take responsibility for how we react to all our experiences and not play the role of victim. Blame is the weakest of emotions. When we don't take responsibility for our experiences of love, we give away all our power.

How do we take responsibility? As I state in *Opening Our Hearts to Men*, the most powerful thing we can do for ourselves when it comes to other people in our lives is to "pick up the mirror instead of the magnifying glass." We do this not to blame ourselves—blame of any kind takes away our power!—but to ask ourselves what it is that we need to learn in order to create the kind of love and life we want. And we move forward from there.

Interesting things happen when we take responsibility for our lives. We lose our anger. We lose our sense of helplessness. We stop being a victim. We gain self-respect. We gain peace of mind. We open our heart. We learn the meaning of love. As we cut away everything that doesn't look like love and replace it with everything that does look like love, how wonderful all our relationships become.

As you read *Love Sweeter Love*, think about your own life and make a long list of all those things that you can do to bring more love into your relationships, whatever the circumstances. And then, step-by-step, take action. This is taking responsibility for your life.

Remember to have patience. Knowing the meaning of love is a lifelong process. But with every step it gets better and better and better. Begin the process now.

Susan Jeffers

# INTRODUCTION

We are all looking for love.

And most of us want it right now.

In this age of instant gratification—McSatisfaction—we forget that intimacy, connection, and abiding love are products of patience. It takes years to know someone, to appreciate his or her strong points rather than focus on weaknesses, to trust enough to share who we truly are.

And yet we're all so blasted busy! How do I find the time, you wonder, not only to work on my relationship but even to enjoy the person I love best?

The answer: Simplify.

In *Home Sweeter Home: Creating a Haven of Simplicity and Spirit*, we looked at ways of uncluttering our homes, slowing our frenetic pace, and freeing our time and energy to place precious people ahead of material things.

In *Love Sweeter Love*, we focus on the basics of relationships. We learn to make them work better through simple principles and explore ways to savor them through good times and bad.

More than ever, we need to look at what really matters in life—the big picture. And what matters most, of course, is relationships.

Too often, we dwell on the complexities of love. When love disappoints us, we might grow disillusioned, even bitter. We might wonder why we always date duds—or swear off the getting-to-know-you scene altogether.

We decide our mate has tricked us—he or she is no longer the individual we married. Or maybe we picked the wrong person. Perhaps sexual interest slowly fades; we settle for companionship instead.

Or we toss it in, the better to find true love elsewhere. Hey, getting divorced is no big deal—doesn't everybody? So we split and discover love anew—only to find the whole insane cycle begins again with a brand-new set of complications.

What a far cry from those movies of the '50s, where boy-meets-girl, boy-and-girl fall in love within five minutes, boy-and-girl marry and become dad-and-mom! Wouldn't it be wonderful if we could stay together and film a sequel with the same characters? Boy-and-girl turned grampa-and-gramma!

Yet we can't go back to the '50s—nor would those of us who lived through them want to!

But we can continue to simplify our lives and our relationships by deciding what and who matters most, setting priorities, working together, and appreciating life's sweet moments.

After two marriages, years of writing about relationships and psychology, interviewing experts, and guiding grown children and friends through the romantic landscape, I've learned that love indeed gets us through the rough spots. But only if we don't give up on love.

*Love Sweeter Love: Creating Relationships of Simplicity and Spirit* is a blend of expert advice, the experiences of ordinary people, and insights from my eventful life, personal and professional.

After reading this gentle, loving, yet realistic guide, you'll feel reassured that the love you seek can be yours. You'll discover that maintaining a mutually satisfying relationship takes work and come away with practical solutions for making it work. You'll realize that your problems are not unique but are similar to those others have anguished over and even solved. You'll find the courage to try again.

As theologian Martin Luther wrote in 1569, "There is no more lovely, friendly, and charming relationship, communion, or company than a good marriage."

You can have the romantic and lasting partnership you desire. Read on . . .

# I. Looking for Mr./Ms. Right: Dating

*Don't compromise yourself. You are all you've got.*
—Janis Joplin

Over and over, we hear that Mr. Right (or Ms. Right) won't come knocking on our door.

Wrong.

My second husband did. Walked right up to my front door and knocked. I was hosting a party for mutual friends. He was invited but didn't plan to come until a friend urged, "Go. You'll like Jann. She's sort of the cheerleader type."

Most profitable party I ever had. It changed my life—and his.

Most of us, however, have to work harder to find our soul mates. The journey can be tedious, hilarious, disillusioning, and even heartbreaking. A sense of humor helps.

Perhaps the journey is toughest in our teens, when love is new and we haven't discovered that we can survive heartbreak.

Eventually we reach a point where we're grateful about all those encounters that didn't work out. Would we really have wanted to be stuck with that person for life?

And with each individual we date—for a month or a year—we learn more about ourselves. We make memories, both silly and sweet.

And we're one person closer to meeting our soul mate.

## MEETING THE RIGHT ONE

I won the lottery of love when the right person showed up on my porch. You might want to paint the front door and plant some welcoming daffodils around the steps—just in case. But as the old saying goes, "Pray, but row toward shore." Getting out and meeting folks is far more effective than answering every doorbell while decked out in your biggest smile.

Some how-to-meet-your-mate experts urge you to plan a strategy: Push yourself to get out several times a week. Ask people you know to introduce you to other singles. Sign up for introduction services. Place personals ads. Force yourself to flirt. Go where wealthy singles are.

Behind this mating frenzy, I sense desperation. And desperation is not an attractive quality. If we're desperate to meet someone, we'll too often settle for less, compromise our values, and be taken advantage of by opportunists who easily ferret out a victim.

I favor the go-about-your-business approach. Do what you love and open yourself to conversations with others doing the same thing. Even if you don't meet anyone, you'll still have a great time while absorbed in an activity you enjoy. You won't lose a thing.

Consider these points:

- Tell friends and family you want to meet people. Accept invitations to gatherings where you know there'll be strangers.

- The more you follow your bliss, the more likely you will meet like-minded people. Go to church or inspirational talks. Join a group that hikes, bikes, or skis. Take night classes in subjects that interest you. Volunteer for a favorite cause. Get involved in the community by joining neighborhood associations and crime watches.

- When someone attracts you, don't wait for that person to do the asking. Send out feelers, then directly ask, "I'm going to see a film tomorrow evening. Would you like to join me?"

- Don't be afraid to stand out. Wear bright or funky clothes that you're comfortable with. Bring your *I Ching* to the party instead of the requested dessert. Offer to share your picnic with that fisherman. Take two signs to a rally, and give one to someone interesting. Be creative and imaginative.

- If you haven't dated in a while, ease in gently by participating in group activities.

- Take a solo vacation where others will be—especially an adventure trip (rafting, a covered-wagon trip, trekking) or special-interest tours (museums, language study, writers' retreats, etc.).

- Don't screen out people too soon. We all want to be loved for who we are, yet we dismiss similar traits in others when we decide within thirty seconds that they're not our type. Give it time!

**KEEP IT SIMPLE: Risk a little to meet Mr./Ms. Right.**

## Try Nondating

If your love life isn't developing the way you'd like, perhaps it's time to do things differently.

But don't flashback to the antiquated 1950s with the let's-trap-a-man mentality of the best-seller *The Rules*: Don't stare at men or talk too much. Stop dating him if he doesn't buy you a romantic gift for your birthday or Valentine's Day. Don't meet a man halfway or go Dutch on a date. Don't call him, and seldom return his calls.

The time is long past for such thinking. You might as well check to see if your stocking seams are straight and your white gloves are fresh. Such "rules" are insulting to both men and women.

Finding a mate—either for men or women—cannot supersede becoming your own person and following your passion. If it does, you wind up married all right—but to a person with whom you either have nothing in common or with whom you can never feel free to be yourself.

As therapist and author Barbara De Angelis points out, the use of manipulation and masquerade prevents us from developing genuine confidence. If love hinges on who someone else thinks we are rather than who we truly are, we are never powerful, merely dependent on tricks.

Now's the time to ditch old thinking and old rules. Techniques Gramma and Grampa used—or the ones we tried as teenagers—need to be updated to fit the times and our new maturity.

Call it "nondating."

What is a nondate? To people who see you and a new "someone" with your heads bent over dinner, it may look like you're on a regular date. But the difference between a date and a nondate is clear to you: Nondating is a different mind-set, a new way of having relationships.

Consider these suggestions:

- Pay your own way and meet the person at your destination, rather than one picking up the other. This helps eliminate the teenage dating pattern and puts you on an equal footing without obligation.

- Talk about the things you're interested in, rather than only drawing out your partner. Divide the conversation evenly between you. Women who heed the lopsided admonition to "talk about him" may wind up dating—or worse yet, married to—someone with whom they have zilch in common.

- You may feel sexual attraction—chemistry—but set it aside and get to know each other, rather than allowing the attraction to govern your actions. Equating lust with love sets you up for disillusion and heartbreak.

- Focus on whether you like the person instead of wondering how the other regards you. In your desire to be liked and loved, you can become so involved in impression management—trying to win approval—that you don't consider if you're having a good time, or even if you like the person with whom you're spending time.

- Stay in the "now," rather than wondering if this evening might "lead to something." Have you ever sat across from a first-time, brown-eyed date wondering if your children would have his or her eyes? Friendships develop at their own pace and because of shared good times, a series of happy "nows." A love relationship has a better chance of developing and lasting if you stay in the "now" instead of projecting yourself into the future.

- Relate to this person as you would to a platonic friend. How do you behave with your pals? You're honest, and you're not afraid to be yourself. If you want to have as satisfying a relationship with a potential love as you do with your best friends, apply the same rules. On the other hand, don't accept behavior in a date you wouldn't stand for in a friendship.

- When you part at the end of the evening, know that it will be OK if and when you see each other again, rather than obsessing on when the other will call. Since the invention of the telephone, men have been saying, "I'll give you a call," and women have been wondering, "When?" If you've ever changed your plans because someone might call or stewed over whether you should be the initiator, it's time to give up control and allow things to happen in their own good time— just as with friends.

- Let several months pass before becoming sexually involved. How many potential relationships have you ruined when you hopped into bed prematurely, leaving you with the disappointment that this person was "just like all the others"? If you wait until you really know and care for the person, sex is more likely to have meaning and less likely to end the relationship.

Nondating may squelch "love at first sight," but it might give love a chance to grow. And if it doesn't, you're still ahead. You can never have too many friends.

**KEEP IT SIMPLE: Try some new "rules."**

## TRAPS SET FOR SINGLES

Ever get the feeling that looking for love is just eighth grade all over again with crow's feet?

Whether we're twenty-two and looking for a lifelong mate, or fifty-two and considering giving love another chance, we can fall into the traps that seem to be set for singles:

*Looking in the wrong places.* Bars attract not only social drinkers but also those who abuse and depend on alcohol. Abusers and alcoholics are not good bets for a satisfying relationship, so finding a different social scene might improve our odds of meeting a healthy person.

We are often advised to go where other men or women gather—often for an activity or class in which we have no interest. If we meet someone there, it's under false pretenses, and we might wind up dating a person whose interests we don't share. If we don't meet anyone, the time spent is a loss. Doesn't it make more sense to do what we love? We'll have a good time whether we meet someone or not.

*Expecting love to solve our problems.* Love may give us someone to enjoy a movie with on Friday night, but it doesn't erase frustrations at work or sadness over family feuding. Love can lend a glow, but nobody else can end our woes. And love usually brings its own problems as we deal with another set of friends, family, personal preferences, and eccentricities—not to mention our lover's problems.

*Confusing sex with love and intimacy.* We all want to feel close to another person, yet many of us confuse physical closeness with emotional closeness. Snuggled in someone's arms, it's easy to pretend that we have loads in common and a future together. But when we get out of bed, we often find that isn't true. Intimacy doesn't come instantly; there are no shortcuts. It takes time to know, trust, and love someone. Sex is not a satisfying substitute— and it can sabotage a relationship. Perhaps we need to act differently and stop jumping into bed.

*Plunging into another relationship.* How many times have we lined up someone new before actually breaking up the current relationship? Look at the people who remarry within months of divorcing. As painful as being alone can be after a breakup, this solitude is necessary in order to feel our feelings, examine what went wrong, decide what we want for our lives, and sort out what's important to us in a future relationship. When we spend our free time looking for someone else and then leap into love, we're probably avoiding a painful growing period. And unless we grow, we're likely to pick the same kind of person the next time and make the same old mistakes. If we don't know ourselves, how can anyone else?

*Moving too fast.* Just as we jump the gun on intimacy with sex, so might we rush into a serious relationship before we're ready. We want so much for this to work out that we take on too much too soon. We spend the weekend together after one date, move in after a month. We might even convince ourselves that this is love at first sight. But do we really know this person? Or are we taking our image of love and projecting it onto him or her? When we do this, we're invariably hurt and disappointed when the real person begins to emerge.

It makes more sense to proceed slowly, as we do with a same-sex friend. (We wouldn't strike up a conversation in the restroom and invite that person home for the weekend, would we?) If the friendship doesn't grow into love, well, we've got a new friend.

*Repeating old patterns without realizing it.* When we've been disappointed repeatedly, we might dismiss all men as jerks or all women as selfish—which doesn't leave us much hope of meeting someone we can be happy with. If things always seem to turn out the same way, we might need to examine our actions. After all, we're the one common thread in all these wrecked relationships. We don't need to keep shooting ourselves in the foot. If we continue to attract men who abuse us or women who take advantage of us, we need to learn why—or things will never change.

**KEEP IT SIMPLE: If your current dating relationship feels familiar, you're probably following the same old destructive pattern.**

## TEENS IN LOVE: IT'S TRICKY

Seventeen-year-old Alan stretches out on the couch at the family gathering and puts his head in girlfriend MaryAnn's lap.

The eighteen-year-old girl strokes his hair dutifully a few times, then hunches her shoulder, trying to move away. He snuggles closer. She hunches even more.

This young couple's prom is a week away—two proms, actually, because they attend separate high schools. They'll be hitting both dances the same night in a $400 limo Alan can't afford. She can't scrape up the money for her dress; Alan's paying for that, too.

The relationship is becoming increasingly one-sided.

This couple has been dating for eight months. They've become sexually active. They've talked about marriage, even though both plan to attend college. But lately, MaryAnn's begun seeing an old boyfriend—platonically, she says. But Alan is worried.

And the more he worries, the more needy and generous he becomes. The more attentive Alan is, the more MaryAnn inches away.

As Alan's aunt, I watch the familiar scene unfold, and my heart goes out to both teenagers.

Careful, Sweetie, I want to tell Alan. Don't let your heart be broken. Realize that you can't buy love. Know that crushing another soul to you too tightly can drive that person from your arms.

MaryAnn, don't tie yourself down too soon, I long to say. Whether Alan likes it or not, now is the time to test your wings, to experiment with who you are becoming.

Bush is blaring from the car radio now instead of Chuck Berry, but teenage love doesn't change.

Dear Alan and MaryAnn—and especially you other younger teens wading into the sea of love—listen to someone who cares. And someone who's been there.

Sexual intimacy is one of life's most delicious rewards. But sex isn't a substitute for television.

Using sex as recreation or entertainment will break your heart, lower your self-esteem, and harm your reputation. Even worse, it might give you a life-threatening disease or affect your life forever with a teenage pregnancy. (Think it'd be easy to have an abortion? Give the baby up for adoption? Raise it yourself? Just ask women who've done it how "easy" it was!)

But you're madly in love, you say, and you're willing to accept the consequences of being sexually active?

As delicious as it seems, sex will sabotage your relationship.

Even if the worst consequences don't happen, sex might preclude talking, having fun together, or socializing with friends. One person might feel used. You both might feel guilty—and certainly worried about pregnancy.

Just as you wouldn't build a bonfire in the living room, you're wise to postpone sex until you're in love with someone of whom your family approves and you'd consider marrying. Wait until you have the maturity and financial independence to live with the consequences. Celibacy until marriage is an option more and more young people are taking. Why mess up your youth—or your whole life—for a fleeting thrill?

It's tempting to give all to love to the exclusion of sports, friends, activities, jobs, and even family. We can become so involved with the relationship, we forget who we are and what we enjoy! You've certainly seen friends become clinging blobs.

Maintaining a sense of self while loving another person is a lifelong balancing act—and tough when love is new. Love should add to our total life experience rather than subtract from it. Here are some questions to ask yourself: Do I still see friends? Are there things I enjoy doing without my steady? Do I feel like I'm giving up who I am for the sake of the relationship? Beware of the smother-lover who wants to monopolize your time or own you. That's not love; that's the other person's insecurity.

Loosen your grip on each other. Broken hearts heal. Sure, you might marry, but chances are greater you'll simply become a life-long memory.

And that, Sweetie, isn't a bad thing to be.

**KEEP IT SIMPLE:** Give your heart—but save yourself.

## Romantic Lightning Can Strike Twice

Sometimes, love takes a long time coming.

On page nine of their 1927 high-school yearbook, Ralph Lindholm's photo is adjacent to Irene Farley's, both somber in the black-and-white tone of the day. In a class of just sixteen, they couldn't help but know one another.

Years passed. Irene stayed in the small town and married class-mate Wayne Bozarth, a dairyman. Ralph moved to a big city, became a fireman, and wed Ruth. Children arrived, and both couples settled into the struggles and joys of married life.

Twice over fifty-one years, Ralph and Irene saw each other at class reunions, chatted with the spouses, and said good-bye. Then, after thirty-eight years together, Irene's husband suffered a fatal heart attack in 1969. Nine years later, Ralph lost his wife of forty-three years to cancer.

Irene kept busy with the house, her four children, and community activities. But like so many men, Ralph felt lost: "My true love was gone, and so was my interest in life." His daughter urged him to check out the ladies at church; he found "zilch on one hand and zero on the other."

And then Ralph saw Irene's byline in their hometown newspaper; she reported news of the community center. He'd heard she was widowed. Something tickled him, way down deep. Dressed in his Sunday clothes and quaking like a schoolboy, he drove to the old hometown and called Irene from the phone booth next to the firehouse.

He played coy. Did she know who this was? Of course not. Remember 1927? Of course—the year she graduated from high school. Did she now know who this was? "I sure do," Irene replied. "There's only two guys left from our class, and the other wouldn't have the nerve to call. So you're Ralph Lindholm."

Could he visit? He could. She opened the door, wondering where his wife was. He gulped; she's even cuter than she was in high school.

One year later, they were married. At what age? "Oodley whump—let's see," muses Irene, thinking hard. She was seventy and he was sixty-nine.

"The greatest blessing is how I've been accepted by all her family—they think I'm the greatest guy in the world," says a happy Ralph, now "Grandpa" to eleven grandchildren, twelve great-grandchildren, and one great-great-grandchild.

Given a second wind by love, Ralph and Irene jumped into civic affairs. She got involved with the garden club, church and community center, Lions Club, the Chamber of Commerce, Toastmasters, United Way, and high-school boosters. Blessed with his fireman's pension, the Lindholms have put out fires before they start by donating $10,000 to the high school and establishing two annual scholarships of $1,000.

A grateful student body honored Ralph with a big "W" sports letter—just like those won by Irene's first husband, Wayne Bozarth. "He was one of my heroes—a great athlete," Ralph recalls. "And he was a good friend of mine—though I don't know if he would've been if he'd known someday I'd marry his wife!"

After fifteen years of marriage, Ralph has had several heart attacks. Irene has trouble negotiating stairs. Time has consigned them to home.

Twice blessed, they tally the secrets of a happy marriage: Never play around. Think things over. Accept the differences between you. Count on the Lord to help straighten things out.

"I love her so much, I can't stand it," says Ralph unabashedly. "She saved my life."

"I was so fortunate to marry two fine men," adds Irene. "I can't believe how happy I am. The Lord has indeed blessed me, and I don't know why."

And so the Lindholms sit in matching recliners beneath a picture of Christ, with dueling television remotes in their hands.

Radio music from another room wafts in, competing with the squawking police/fire scanner and television. Come 8 P.M., they head for bed, holding hands as they fall asleep with their miniature poodle, Duke, between them.

Now in their mid-eighties, the Lindholms are as comfy as a couple who've known one another all their lives. Which they have.

Though love was a long time coming.

**KEEP IT SIMPLE: Trust your heart. Make that call.**

## REUNION ROMANCE

Debating whether or not to attend that upcoming class reunion?

Don J. Moisan and Melaney J. Welch both looked forward to attending their ten-year high-school reunion, Class of '67.

She was recently divorced, with two small boys, and was running a flower shop. He was divorced, too, with three little boys. He'd moved from their hometown to run a dairy farm.

Their class was small—just 132. In 1977, the old classmates were in their late twenties, old enough to have experienced heartbreak but young enough to remain optimistic. Don, who never cared much for school, hoped to meet someone at that tenth reunion. But neither he nor Melaney remembered each other. "Who's that?" Melaney asked a pal when Don walked into the gathering at a pizza parlor. "We didn't go to school with him."

Seven months later, they married.

Reunions might just be a good bet for romance. After all, you grew up together. You know the person's background. You're the same age. You already have common friends. Growing up in the same time and place, you may share similar values.

Don and Melaney's similarities—as well as their values and beliefs as Christians—cemented their romance quickly. "It made me wish I'd known her in high school," Don says. "At the reunion, I pretty much fell in love with her from the beginning."

Now in their forties, Don continues as a dairy farmer, and Melaney is a university public-relations person. They've added a son and a daughter to the five boys they first shared. The Moisans urge others to attend their school reunions. Even if romance doesn't result, reconnecting with old friends is meaningful in this fast-paced, transient society.

And perhaps Cupid—that little arrow-slinger who never changes—will attend, too.

**KEEP IT SIMPLE: Say yes to that reunion invitation.**

# 2. TYING THE KNOT: WEDDINGS

*When a man loves a woman and that woman loves him, the angels leave heaven and come to their house and sing.*
—Brahma

Have you ever cried at a wedding?

I certainly have—even at a wedding of strangers when I chanced across an elaborate cathedral ceremony while vacationing in Mexico.

We weepers recall the bride and groom's tender love story, his clever proposal, her feigned surprise. We may remember them as children and marvel at the swift passage of time. Perhaps we recall other weddings, other love stories.

And we flash ahead to all the joys—and travails—awaiting this eager couple, oblivious to all but each other at this delightful time.

To better prepare for their big day and their future together, many couples seek premarital counseling. Others form contracts or write the vows they will make to one another. In this chapter, you'll even meet a couple who extended their wedding to include rituals performed throughout the year.

If you know a couple planning marriage, buy another copy of this book and present it as a shower or engagement gift—with this chapter marked.

## LETTER TO AN ENGAGED DAUGHTER

*My darling daughter*:

Congratulations on your engagement! How joyous it was to hear your news and feel so good about the fine young man you have chosen.

At twenty-seven, you are much better equipped to marry than I was at eighteen. You know who you are and what you want; I got married so I wouldn't have to decide.

You identified the things in life that were holding you back and tackled them head-on; I hadn't a clue.

You returned to college determined to finish; I skipped my history final to choose wedding shoes.

Obviously, I wasn't a young woman to emulate. But the years have taught me a few things, aided by the endless weddings (and divorces) I've witnessed and the countless experts I've interviewed.

Please indulge my advice-giving:

*Don't get so caught up in the fun of wedding planning that you forget what the engagement is.* It's a glorious flurry of choices right now. It's fun sharing it all with you, like in the first days after your birth when I'd ask you aloud if you wanted your bath or your nap first. But the most important decisions you have to make now are with your bridegroom, and they stretch far beyond the big day. Now is the time for some "home" work.

Will you help each other reach your goals? Can you agree on the religious beliefs that will guide your children? Are you secure enough with each other to fight—and mature enough to fight fairly? Can you divide household chores so that neither of you feels burdened? Are you willing to seek professional help when you can't solve problems yourselves? Can you compromise about participating in family events and have the courage to say no when you want to start your own traditions? And even though you've lived with your parents' divorce, are you entering marriage without that option as an easy out?

*Remember that a wedding should be joyous, not perfection.* The bridal magazines coo "perfection"—as if that's possible. How hard couples work to have a perfect wedding, even spending themselves—or their parents!—into debt for just the right colors, tears if the cake is late, and even hard feelings among relatives if their children aren't welcome.

A wedding is a celebration with real people, not a magazine ad with posed models. That means something will go awry (and you'll laugh for years about it), childish voices or the cries of the newest family members will be audible on the videotape, and somebody's aunt is going to put her foot in her mouth again. People—not colors, or roses, or hors d'oeuvres—are what's important. Someday you'll look back fondly at your photos and count those who are no longer here. Each precious person will stand out in your memory, and you'll forget that the bridesmaids' shoes didn't quite match the mints.

*It's all right to change your mind.* As she was adjusting my veil, my mother said, "Honey, it's all right if you want to change your mind." Deep inside, I knew that might be a wise idea, but the church was full of people. Although we divorced eight years later, you and your brother and sister wouldn't be here if I'd heeded Mom's invitation. I'm glad I plunged ahead.

But the reminder bears repeating. Although I've written some hefty deposit checks, even when you're walking down the aisle, it isn't too late to step back and consider whether marriage is truly what you want. The world is full of divorce statistics from couples who never paused to reflect. I'd rather lose some money—and perhaps be embarrassed—than have you wind up one of that number.

Think on these things, my dear daughter, and talk them over with your groom. Plan ahead, have fun, and keep things in perspective.

*Love, Mom*

P.S. Which strikes your fancy: the midnight-blue carriage with one horse, or the white Cinderella coach with the footman?

**KEEP IT SIMPLE: Love matters. Details don't.**

## GREEN WEDDINGS

When Carol Jones and Steve Reed married during the summer of 1993, they wanted two things—besides each other. They needed a wedding that reflected their values, that was environmentally sound and simple. And they needed a compromise between their first weddings to others—his a big traditional ceremony, hers a hippie do with a potluck in a park. The couple agreed on an outdoor ceremony in a state park overlooking Washington's Puget Sound. Thirty-two of the fifty invited guests showed up.

Instead of formal invitations, they sent recycled-paper cards with a picture resembling the site. Carol wore a $70, off-the-rack white brocade suit, wearable for other occasions. A flower girl was the only attendant, scattering rose petals from Carol's sister's garden. Guests made corsages and bouquets from $60 worth of flowers from the local grocery store—plenty for table arrangements, the reception, and for guests to take home. Carol intended to make the cake but got sick; she ordered a $35 grocery-store cake at the last minute. The biggest expense of the $2,500 wedding was the brunch buffet reception at a historic, antique-filled hotel.

As nice as it was, there are things forty-one-year-old Carol would have done differently, which is why she passes on what she's learned in a book, *Green Weddings That Don't Cost the Earth*, and the *Green Weddings Newsletter* (see Resources).

Carol is a music teacher and children's author who's always loved nature; her tenth birthday party was a canteen-toting hike with guests. Steve, thirty-seven, is an environmental activist.

"It's a craze when you begin planning your wedding," Carol recalls. "You read all these wedding planning books, find all these picky details—really interesting, but none had anything about the type of stuff I wanted to do."

If she were marrying today, Carol would stay well so she could bake that cake—and she tells you how in the book. She'd make the brunch vegetarian and would specify recyclable food, bottles, and cardboard in the catering contract.

"A wedding is the beginning of a new phase in our lives," Carol says. "As you're learning to live as a couple, you can also learn to do things for the environment." To Carol, a "green" wedding or life means living in harmony with the earth and others.

Here are some suggestions for natural nuptials:

*Candles.* Candles contain paraffin, a petroleum product. Be earth-friendly with beeswax candles—or even olive-oil lamps.

*Flowers.* Marry outdoors and let nature provide decorations. Save beaucoup de bucks by carrying one flower or a simple arm bouquet of long-stemmed flowers tied with a ribbon. In-season flowers are cheaper, and if from a friend's yard, even more so. Dry your bouquet, or use a rooting hormone to sprout it. One woman gave her sister a dozen rose bushes on her first anniversary, grown from the roses in her bouquet.

*Gifts.* Avoid unneeded gifts by including a list of environmental organizations and favorite charities with your invitations and suggest a donation in lieu of gifts.

*The getaway.* Forget the gas-guzzling limo and be creative. One couple rode off on a tandem bike with a JUST MARRIED sign and tin cans.

*Food.* Put green consumerism to work with a vegetarian reception—organic, locally grown, and in-season, to make it truly PC. Donate uneaten food to a homeless shelter.

*Honeymoon.* Green up your honeymoon by vacationing locally. Or, consider an ecotour, which funnels money back into the local economy and respects local resources.

**KEEP IT SIMPLE: Weddings needn't cost a fortune.**

## REALISTIC VOWS

We've all been to weddings that make us cry. Weddings that make us wonder whether it will last. Weddings that come off perfectly. Weddings that make us giggle when something goes wrong.

But how many of us have attended a ceremony that made us wish the vows were a petition we could sign?

The September 1990 wedding of Nikki and Bob Cassidy was like that. Their vows, penned themselves, were so specific and so basic—so pertinent to reality—that many of the guests were nodding their heads in agreement. I heard at least one "Right on!" and thought "Write on..."

Like many of us, Bob and Nikki were each marrying for a second time. In their fifties, they both have grown children and grandchildren. They are from different religions. And both are working hard at recovery from alcoholism. In fact, both have worked in the treatment field.

Their vows not only reflected their circumstances but also the precepts they follow to ensure their sobriety and live satisfying lives.

No matter what people's circumstances are, these vows are worth considering for those who are in—or who hope to have—a lasting relationship. They're not traditional; they *are* guidelines to a healthy union.

In addition to promising fidelity and eternal love and friendship, Bob and Nikki made these vows (I added my comments):

## TOGETHERNESS

*I promise to communicate directly and honestly with you.* When we don't say what we're really thinking or feeling because we fear our partner's reaction, we're preventing them from really knowing us.

*I promise to recognize that we will have differences of opinion and that we are both entitled to our own opinions.* How easy it is to fall into the "if you really loved me you'd agree" trap. Agreeing that we don't have to agree takes a burden off the relationship.

*I promise not to do for you what you can do for yourself.* This doesn't mean omitting little niceties; it refers to having faith in our partner's ability to solve his or her own problems and take care of his or her own life.

*I promise to listen to your needs. I promise to tell you about my needs.* Spouses aren't mind readers. When we determine what we need and ask for it, those we love are usually happy to grant it.

*I promise to keep you as the most important person in my life. You shall be my priority in all things.* Putting the kids, work, or even the newspaper or television ahead of our spouse can easily happen unless we make a conscious effort otherwise.

*I promise to listen to you and stay emotionally available in times of adversity as well as prosperity.* Being there for someone else—even when we're tired, bored, or preoccupied—is sure proof of love.

*I promise when I am wrong to admit it, and, with God's help, to change.* It takes a big person to say, "I was wrong," but it sure smoothes the marital path.

## PARENTHOOD

*I promise to be available to your children.* Extending love, time, and attention to another person's children isn't always convenient, but it's one of the greatest gifts we can give to someone we love. And the kids profit, too.

*I promise to do what I can to maintain a loving relationship between our children and our life, sharing with you the joys and sorrows of being a parent and supporting you in all matters.* Biological parents often disagree over child-rearing; stepparents will too. But stepparents can offer valuable insights, free of emotional baggage. A healthy spouse is secure enough to allow the other time alone with his or her children.

## SPIRITUALITY

*I promise not to interfere with your spiritual journey or with your religious practices, respecting you as having another journey with God, apart from me.* A saying in some therapy circles goes, "What you think is none of my business." This also applies to religion, for what is more personal than one's spiritual path? It's something a loving mate will honor, not refute or envy.

**KEEP IT SIMPLE: Tailor your vows to suit your situation.**

# FIRST-YEAR RITUALS

On December 1994, Kate McKern and Doug Verigin married in front of their fireplace with a handful of friends and his two kids.

On March 18, 1995, they did it again—a big blowout with two hundred people at Portland's Scottish Rite Temple.

On June 17, 1995, they traveled to Iowa for a fete by her family and friends.

On September 23, 1995, they asked the original wedding guests to their home for the year's fourth and final wedding ritual—a celebration of sowing and reaping.

Boy, are they married!

This couple is not only hooked on each other but on ritual—essential, they say, to celebrating, honoring, and remembering.

"Life is so fast now, and when we move so quickly, we miss what we're feeling and what's happening in nature," says Kate. "Ritual demands you be in the moment."

That's why they punctuated their first year of married life with what they call "a series of nuptial events."

Getting married is exciting—especially when you wait until you're forty-four to do it, Kate reasons. But then comes the letdown. And she didn't want that to happen; they wanted to sustain their love and jubilance.

"Each time we do our personal vows, it takes us deeper into each other," says Kate, a former television producer and publicist who's now a minister performing rituals for women.

"And into ourselves," adds Doug, who runs a market-research firm. "You start to recognize a little different meaning in what you're saying as you go through the experience of being married. The shades of meaning become deeper. Different facets become apparent."

Both believe that community is essential to marriage and family. Each ritual celebrated community, with friends contributing a catered wedding dinner after the first service and floral arrangements with a wedding-cake-shaped piñata at the second.

The initial wedding invitation asked friends to "a celebration of marriage and the joyful creation of a family group." His young children, Justine and Tyler, played pivotal roles in each ceremony.

"We wanted to make sure they understood we were creating a new family group but not imposing on their relationship with their mother," says Doug.

In the vows she has repeated to the children at each of the rituals, Kate has told them that they already have both a mother and father, and that she's here to be their angel—to help watch over them and make their dreams come true. At the first ceremony, she gave them hand-blown glass animals; at the second, small fuzzy animals; at the third, little dream-catchers she made.

Kate became interested in ritual when she reached forty. She wanted a ceremony that was personally empowering. Relying on her television-producing, spirituality, and theater skills, she devised a ritual that included eight women friends.

Today she has her own company, Rituals by Design, in Portland, Oregon. She has created ceremonies for house blessings, bridal showers, anniversaries, pet funerals, separations, and transfers of business ownership—and now monthly "moon ceremonies" celebrating the support of women for each other.

Rituals are an integral part of the Verigin household.

While courting, Doug and Kate held several rituals, including—when things were looking serious—a thirty-day commitment to stay in the relationship, followed by a sixty-day, then ninety-day, commitment.

"That was not only about the future," says Doug, "but about resolving and releasing the past."

The couple has also begun a last-day-of-school tradition with the kids. They take the children to breakfast and let them order anything they want. They give the kids symbolic presents and design certificates for them. And the chaos of routine school mornings is quieted momentarily with a breakfast blessing in which the family holds hands, says a prayer, and sends positive energy to each other. Sometimes the adults ask the kids what they need a blessing for on that day and then bestow one.

At each of the wedding rituals, they repeated vows written for one another. This is part of Kate's vows:

In this moment now, I honor your commitment to your spiritual path. It has awakened the Goddess in me.

I marvel at your devotion to your children. It has awakened the mother in me.

I delight in your delight of sensual pleasures. It has awakened the woman in me.

And I rejoice at your desire for a life partner. It has awakened the wife in me.

Awakening.
That's part of what marriage—and ritual—are about.

**KEEP IT SIMPLE:** Add meaning to your union by repeating your vows occasionally.

# May-December Unions

There's no law that says thirty-year-olds must fall in love with other thirty-year-olds. Most people marry within a five-year age range simply because they usually associate with folks in the same age bracket.

But times are changing.

## Older Women, Younger Men

Men long have had the option of marrying women who are far younger. They often do, especially in subsequent marriages.

Women now are exercising that option, citing equality as a top aspect of such unions. Younger men seem to be less threatened by a woman's independence, they say.

In *Loving a Younger Man: How Women Are Finding and Enjoying a Better Relationship*, Victoria Houston explores the phenomenon. She's married to a man nine years her junior, after sixteen years with a husband who didn't want a career-oriented wife.

Victoria uses statistics to torpedo the notion that women's chances of marrying decrease as they age (because the pool of same-age eligible men declines). In fact, a third of American women are living with or marrying men who are younger.

She contends that many women ignore the younger-man option because they've bought the old-boy rule against it. Loving a younger man is not only possible but often works well, according to the couples she interviewed, who have been together from three to twenty years.

Two women who've chosen younger men are actress Patty Duke (Michael Pearce, her fourth husband, is seven years her junior) and Stephanie McCaleb, a California credit-union executive (her boyfriend of many years, Joseph Amaral, is five and one-half years younger).

"There's something very affirming about knowing you're attractive to someone this age," Patty Duke says. "I feel wonderful that this young, healthy, gorgeous man who could have any young woman he wants finds me sexy." But more than that is the sense of equality: "I've done 'Daddy' twice," Patty says.

Like Patty, Stephanie had married two slightly older men but finds that the two younger ones she has dated "treat me as an equal. They listen to me and don't patronize me. Younger men who grew up during the '60s have a different attitude toward women; they really understand the concept of equality."

Loving a younger man can bring some insecurity. Patty says that sometimes she'll ask her husband to put on a suit to look more mature "because I feel old next to him. The fact I feel free to ask shows the strength of this relationship. There was a time when I would have held it in and picked a fight about something else."

Being better established financially can be confusing for "older women": "I grew up thinking he's supposed to have more money, that I gained my status from the financial capabilities of my partner," Stephanie says.

"When we Dutch treat, part of me says that's not the way it's supposed to be, while part says when somebody else is paying for everything, you pay quite a price in the long run. My second husband made $150,000 a year, and I was miserable. This is such a better relationship," Stephanie concludes, "in terms of how I'm treated."

## OLDER MEN, YOUNGER WOMEN

What does skater Nancy Kerrigan have in common with model Rachel Hunter? Besides fame and money, they've both married older men. Business manager Jerry Solomon is fifteen years older than Nancy. Rocker Rod Stewart has twenty-four years on Rachel.

Worldwide, husbands tend to be two to six years older than their wives. In the United States, age differences increase with remarriage, because divorced men tend to marry younger women. Yet May-December unions are nothing new. Ted Kennedy is twenty-two years older than second wife Victoria Reggie. Hugh Hefner has thirty-seven years on wife Kimberley Conrad.

I can relate. Most of my significant relationships, including both husbands, have been from eight to twenty-seven years older.

Such pairings are perennially popular. So much so that a national organization, Wives of Older Men, was founded in 1988 for couples with more than eight years' disparity in age (see Resources).

Anthropologists find historical reasons for this behavior from humankind's earliest days. Women were attracted to powerful men who could protect them and their young. Early man looked for a young, attractive mate who'd reproduce frequently. For both, mating successfully was a matter of survival.

Biology is still with us; successful, powerful men still attract women easily. Rich or famous wins out over old, fat, and bald. Today an older man may be more confident, have more disposable income, know how to treat a woman, and be a more considerate lover than his younger counterpart. He also may have learned from past relationships, have more time to spend with her instead of spending long hours at work, and be able to serve as her professional mentor. On the downside, he may be an

immature sort who enjoys a woman he can easily impress—
or even subjugate.

"Plus, the younger woman offers him eternal life, the chance to
stay young," points out therapist Mary Lansing, a member of the
American Association for Marriage and Family Therapy. "I think
men are more afraid of aging than women are."

What about the pop-psych stuff concerning father figures?

Many experts point out that we subconciously tend to marry
our parents. Lansing won't go so far as to call attraction to older
men a father complex, but she notes that many such women
were deserted, either physically or emotionally, by their fathers
during childhood.

"Marrying someone older makes up for that existential void,"
Lansing says. "He's someone she can lean on, and—most importantly—who she can get validation from. And when somebody's
twenty or thirty years older, there's a whole lot of comfort there.
Security and a sense of well-being, like you don't need to be afraid."

Yet age disparities can create difficulties.

For women in their twenties and thirties, there's the baby question: She wants to have a baby, but does he?

Lansing finds some women in their mid-fifties skittish about
marrying older men, fearing they'll wind up playing nursemaid.
If the man's retired and she's still working, priorities may be out
of balance. That doesn't mean women should rule out older
men. But Lansing offers a significant caveat: If we don't feel

strong and capable ourselves, we may project those qualities onto the older man.

But some older men are rigid about gender roles, and his care-taking may one day become cloying—or even prevent a woman from growing.

"As you begin to take care of yourself more, you don't need to be validated from the outside," Lansing says. "When a woman finds that inner strength, she doesn't need to project it onto an older man."

And developing self-reliance opens us up to relationships with people of any age.

**KEEP IT SIMPLE: Calendars count years. Hearts don't have to.**

## AFTER-WEDDING WISDOM

Watching a young couple enter a bridal shop recently reminded me of the fun involved in planning a wedding.

I also was reminded how easy it is to get married, even when facing the myriad details, and how difficult it is to stay married.

Especially when we're starting out, it's so much easier to worry about the shade of the bridesmaids' dresses than to jump ahead to anticipating the realities of day-to-day life together.

But which is more important?

Instead of taking a gift to the next wedding I attend (who needs another crystal candy dish?), I'm tempted to take a list of dos and don'ts. It wouldn't be a glamorous gift, but it would be more practical.

Here's how that list would read:

*Let there be spaces in your togetherness.* Poet Kahlil Gibran offered this wise advice. In the first blush of love, a couple tends to want to do everything together. But the closeness that may seem initially endearing can get downright annoying. Everyone needs time alone—and deserves it, without having to explain or justify it. Being soul mates doesn't make you the Bobbsey twins.

*Don't count on changing each other.* Going into marriage with the idea that you'll change the qualities you don't care for in your partner is a mistake. For one thing, most people don't change unless they either want to or are in such great pain that they feel forced to. If you can't stand the way your sweetie eats or talks or treats his mother before the wedding, perhaps it's time to rethink the whole relationship. When the going gets tough, it's tempting to focus on what the other person is doing wrong. But it's infinitely more helpful to consider what each of us can do differently.

*You don't always have to agree.* Love doesn't mean agreeing on everything—although it certainly helps to share the same values. But it does mean respecting the other's opinions. I grew up thinking that if I loved someone, I had to see everything his way. It took me years to unlearn it. Don't try to remake the other individual in your image. Value your differences and enjoy the spice that each of you lends to the relationship.

*Don't compromise yourself into boredom.* Yes, marriage demands compromise and finding solutions you can both live with. But when you're first married, you can be so anxious to please the other that you continually swallow your own preferences to do what the other person wants. If you do it often enough, you get resentful and no longer feel important. Don't try to please the other so hard that you abandon yourself.

*Don't keep score.* Relationships aren't always fifty-fifty. Some days they're seventy to thirty—or maybe even one hundred to zero (as when one of you is sick). Sincere and persistent effort balances out over the years; don't measure it a week at a time.

*Respect each other's boundaries.* A marriage license doesn't give you license to go through each other's drawers, wallets, journals, pockets, or mail. Grant your partner the privacy and respect you want for yourself. (It isn't fair saying, "But I have nothing to hide, so why should my partner mind my snooping?")

*Divvy up the chores—then butt out.* Agree on how you'll handle household duties, but don't appoint yourself overseer. Let your partner handle those tasks in his or her own way.

*Don't tell all.* There's nothing that you can't tell me, but there's also nothing you must tell me. That includes sexual histories and other personal information that could be used as ammunition if the fighting gets unfair. Experts advise revealing only what could affect the other, such as disease, children, prison records, and so forth.

*Accept each other's limitations.* When you find that you constantly criticize your partner, it's often because you're highly self-critical. As you work to accept your personal limitations and realize that you're valuable despite your faults, you can cut your partner some slack.

Sound like a lot of work? It is. In comparison, matching those bridesmaids' dresses is a cinch.

But not as rewarding.

**KEEP IT SIMPLE: It's our job simply to love each other—not to judge, correct, teach, or condemn.**

## BEARING THE WEDDING DAY

Through nearly two decades of days and nights, the bear had been the girl's best companion.

"There's been about a million tears cried on this bear," she'd said at age nine. Today, the girl was nearing twenty, and the bear looked his age. One eye had winked off into nowhere, and the yellow fur had been rubbed thin and brown.

The girl's mother felt as bad as the bear looked. Because today—too soon, the mother thought—the girl was abandoning the bear to become a bride. Now the strong arms of her young Marine husband would soothe her to sleep.

The girl may have been ready to give up the bear, but the mother was not prepared to give up her daughter. Both child and bear had left her home two years ago when the girl moved out on her own—spurred, no doubt, by the fact that the mother had become a bride for a second time herself. The girl and the bear found themselves interlopers.

Now the mother felt estranged. She had not met the eager young man she would soon call son-in-law. She didn't even know his name when the collect call came: "I don't know how to tell you this, Mom, but I'm getting married Monday."

Tears stung the mother's eyes. Not yet—not this way. She pleaded for an engagement, cajoled with talk of a Christmas wedding with colors of silver, white, and the blue the girl had always loved. But the girl was adamant.

It was love. It was now. And it was more than the mother could stand.

She felt hurt and angry at the girl's obliviousness to her feelings. She was wary of a union founded on so little time. She felt manipulated into "blessing" something she could not and cheated out of the big wedding plans that guaranteed nothing yet seemed a mother's birthright.

She was sadly nostalgic, recalling how she, too, had married even younger—an acceptable shortcut to adulthood, a quick escape from having to decide what she wanted to be when she grew up. The mother ached as her mind flashed reruns of broken-home movies.

The mother considered not attending the wedding. Relatives urged her to say no to this willful woman-child who would not wait.

Her brain balked, but her heart knew it would keep the unspecified date made the day the girl was born. The mother boarded the plane with sad acceptance, her string of pearls packed safely to serve as "something borrowed."

She would tell the girl and the Marine—just once—how she felt. Then she would bless them both and hope with all her heart. The battered bear would get one last hug.

Because daughters and sons grow up.

And mothers—like bears—must learn to let go.

**KEEP IT SIMPLE: We must accept our children's choices.**

# 3. FOSTERING TOGETHERNESS: INTIMACY

*Now I want to be with my best friend, and my best friend's my wife. Who could ask for anything more?*
—John Lennon

Intimacy is the simplest, sweetest thing a couple can share. Contrary to popular opinion, sex is not intimacy. A couple must spend years together to develop intimacy.

Intimacy is about trust: Trust that what we say won't be used against us. That our tender spots will be protected. That our secrets won't be broadcast.

Intimacy is also about sharing: tears, laughter, fear, joy. It's weathering the rough spots without drawing apart. It's being able to finish one another's sentences.

Yet intimacy isn't constant togetherness, enmeshment, or control. Intimacy demands boundaries; I know who I am and invite you into the circle of myself. You know who you are, too, and when you choose to be alone or private, I honor that.

One of the most delicious aspects of intimacy is humor. We crack up over the craziest things, share private jokes, talk in our personal code.

Intimacy doesn't happen overnight. But, oh, is it ever worth the wait!

## SHARING CLOSETS

Marriage may be made in heaven, but this couple's union could have ended in the closet.

There they were in the throes of middle-aged love. Eager to share what was left of their lives. In harmony over basic values and willing to give each other what modern couples call "space."

That space did not extend to the closet. Neither did togetherness.

After thirteen years of solitary spreading, she found her clothes consorting with a closetful of macho gear. His T-shirts with their fierce cartoon faces leered above jocular male messages. Cowboy boots stampeded across the floor. Baseball caps toppled from overhead shelves. Belt buckles the size of warriors' shields clanged against the walls.

There was even a saddle grazing in one corner until it was banished to the garage. It was for his horse, but she came across as the nag.

One proposal followed another. He suggested that she keep her clothes in the other bedroom's closet—already bulging with a teenage daughter's football jerseys and formals.

Move out of the master-bedroom closet? The idea was as discriminatory as the identification. There's something illicit and temporary about not dressing in the room you sleep in. A woman's place is in the House, the Senate, and the "master" closet.

The couple had differences to work out.

She was a believer in Goodwill. Before she made the big move, she tried on clothes, then sorted, discarded, and took bagsful to the charity truck at the shopping center. He was a believer in Save-It. The wool jacket he'd bought in Ireland. The African dashikis. The shorts that didn't fit.

"Pack what he doesn't wear in boxes," a friend suggested. "If he doesn't ask for something in six months, pitch it." That didn't seem honest, so instead she organized.

"A place for everything…" she trilled as she folded matching cardboard boxes into under-the-bed and back-of-the-closet storage containers. "And everything in its place," she beamed as she clipped her skirts and hung her blouses on those handy hanger trees that hold one hundred garments in a half-inch of space.

Convenient, it wasn't. But the process did seem, well, cooperative.

He considered her project a pain. There were more important tasks in life than transferring shirts from laundry hangers to hanger trees. And he grimaced when he had to roll to the other side of the bed so she could pull out under-the-bed storage boxes holding her vests.

They were only five months into the marriage and they'd become a triangle—him, her, and the closet. No magazine or talk show addressed this problem. Could this marriage be saved?

Then it happened. She spotted a newspaper ad for closet organizers, do-it-yourself kits on sale for $69. Judging from the picture on the box, a person could assemble those extra shelves and hold a party the same night.

Not so.

But any marriage with wedding gifts still in boxes is worth saving. They plunged into the project with determination. One day's work and several scuffed knuckles later, it was done.

Just like the people in the television commercials, they shared cups of coffee as they sat on the edge of the bed admiring their closet.

All his jackets and shirts on one pole, her skirts and blouses on another. Pants and dresses peacefully sharing a narrower pole for longer items, and shelves of perfectly folded sweaters presiding over the closet center. Shoes neatly aligned across the top shelf and perched on a rack.

It was beautiful. Together they had created a new being that resembled them both.

And it would never require orthodontia.


KEEP IT SIMPLE: Compromise and cooperate, from the closet outward.

## Change the Baby, Not Your Mate

Imagine buying a new car but hoping the interior will look different once you get it home.

Sound crazy? Yet people consistently try to change other people, especially their mates. Experts say this behavior is destructive—and futile—for several reasons:

- It implies, "You're not OK the way you are."

- It puts the focus on your mate, not you—and you're the only one you can control.

- It makes you prosecutor, judge, and jury—hardly an equal to your partner.

- It leads to controlling your mate.

- It produces resentment.

The tricks to change and control are endless: advising, nagging, scolding, manipulating, checking up on, convincing, comparing, warning, and threatening.

They don't work.

"I don't think you can love under those conditions—you're always sort of raising people like they're a child," says Jennifer James, a Seattle, Washington, author and cultural anthropologist. "If you want acceptance, you have to give it as well."

Herb Goldberg, a Los Angeles psychologist specializing in men, notes that when women try to change men (and this works both ways), "They're actually trying to get him to satisfy needs he can't. He senses that and closes up.

"Behind every attempt to change him, a man experiences an accusation, a criticism: 'You're not enough of this, you're not enough of that.' He goes in the opposite direction."

Goldberg warns those trying to change a mate: "The person you're attracted to is a direct extension of who you are. So when you try to change somebody else, you're being irresponsible—because you chose that person. The real question to ask yourself is, 'Why did I choose this person?' Changing your partner is one more form of avoiding yourself. The real change has to come in you.

"It's cruel to try to change somebody else. The implication is that their behavior is in a vacuum rather than in response to you," he continues. Self-hating, guilt-ridden people believe you, resulting in "a worse relationship than before."

In his PBS television series on the family, John Bradshaw noted that "control is absolute illusion. Those who try will pay for it someday."

Perhaps this reminder from an unknown author says it best:

TO LET GO does not mean to stop caring. It means I can't do it for someone else.

TO LET GO is not to cut myself off, but the realization I can't control another.

TO LET GO is not to enable, but to allow learning from natural consequences.

TO LET GO is to admit being powerless, which means the outcome is not in my hands.

TO LET GO is not trying to change or blame another, it's making the most of myself.

TO LET GO is not to care for, but to care about.

TO LET GO is not to fix, but to be supportive.

TO LET GO is not to judge, but to allow another to be a human being.

TO LET GO is not to be in the middle arranging all the outcomes, but to allow others to affect their own destinies.

TO LET GO is not to be protective, it's to permit another person to face reality.

TO LET GO is not to criticize or regulate anyone, but to try to become what I dream I can be.

TO LET GO is to fear less and love more.

KEEP IT SIMPLE: You can change only yourself, no one else.

## Precious Privacy

A poll by the *Boston Parents' Paper* shows that privacy and solitude within the family are paramount in parents' minds. Yet many of us are stymied about how to find it. We want to establish quality time as a couple or a family.

But we also need—no matter what our age—time to be alone. And finding a time and a place to be alone isn't easy in a busy household.

There are psychological as well as physical factors.

The psychological aspect is that every family member is entitled to privacy. Healthy families acknowledge and respect others' boundaries. They respect one another's privacy.

Privacy means knocking before opening a closed door. Leaving people alone in the bathroom. Not snooping through drawers and diaries. Not eating that leftover dessert someone has saved for later. Asking before borrowing clothes or another's belongings.

If our boundaries weren't respected as kids—Mom read our diary, our brother barged into the bathroom—it's easy to have a poor sense of boundaries. But if we can remember our frustration, embarrassment, or even outrage at being violated, that's an incentive to establish healthy boundaries today.

Here are some things to consider:

*Let each person have his or her own room or space.* Or at least set aside a special space no one else will plunder: a corner of a room (bedroom, den, garage), closet, shelves, drawers, boxes under the bed. This is equally as vital for children who don't live with us all the time. Having a space of their own, however small, and special belongings that remain at Mom's or Dad's (or the grandparents') assures them they have a permanent place in that person's home and heart.

A space of one's own is especially important for women. Often, women consider all the house their domain—yet there isn't any one place they can call our own. A man often has a workshop in the basement or much of the garage. A woman's space is vital; it helps her retain her wholeness and keeps her in touch with her soul.

Domestic partners may even choose to have separate bedrooms. This doesn't mean they don't sleep together most nights. It simply offers private space in which to be themselves, to be alone with their thoughts—or to separate to cool off, recuperate from illness, or catch up on sleep from snoring-induced sleeplessness.

*Rethink "time out" as punishment.* Are we teaching children that being alone is something undesirable? We might be able to counter this with positive alone time. We can talk about our need to be alone at times and see that the child has regular time to himself or herself.

*Schedule regular quiet time.* This means the television is off while people read, do homework, or work on a hobby or project, together or alone. You may choose to play classical music (which is soothing and introduces the kids to good music), but keep it low. Make quiet time a regular, anticipated part of each evening.

*Secure doors.* Locks on bedroom and bathroom doors signify that the household respects privacy. To prevent toddlers from locking themselves in, use a doorknob that can be easily picked with a bobby pin from the outside—or a chain lock high up that a child can't reach.

*Create a home retreat.* Designate a guest room and assign it periodically to each family member (put a chart outside the door and let them make reservations). Or let a teenager book the family or living room one night to entertain friends.

*Make a special nook.* Create a closet, a nook under the stairs, or a part of the attic as a comfy, cozy, quiet spot in which to read, study, listen to music, write, talk on the phone, or meditate.

Consider erecting a teepee in the family room or playroom. Put up a playhouse or tree house in the yard to accustom children to having a private place.

*Create alone time.* Give parents and older children the treat of being home alone. Partners can give this gift to one another by taking the kids out for an evening or weekend afternoon—or, if there are no kids, going off alone or with a friend. Parents can demonstrate they trust a child by giving them such space.

*Plan parent-child "dates."* Having a parent all to yourself is a treat for children of all ages, and the delights of that particular child are most appreciated when you can focus only on them. Aim for such a night once a month—and encourage private outings for each child with a grandparent, aunt, or uncle. Kids will enjoy a burger out, cruising the mall, a hike in the woods, or a walk to the corner for an ice-cream cone.

Let's remember that solitude and privacy are just as essential as togetherness.

**KEEP IT SIMPLE: We all need time and space alone to nourish our souls.**

## WORKING COUPLES: TIME TOGETHER

When both partners work outside the home, life can feel so frenetic you wonder why you got married in the first place. It may even seem you spent more time together while dating.

Time together is essential to intimacy. And it must be time *together*—not time spent watching the kids play soccer or discussing with Bobby's teacher why he can't grasp algebra. Parents who sacrifice their own relationship for the sake of the kids become empty nesters at home with a stranger.

The business of life can usurp time for intimacy if we don't make it a priority and build it into our lives. "We'll spend time together and enjoy each other when I can get around to it" isn't good enough.

Here are some ways to increase and build intimacy:

*Schedule time together.* This may be a Friday-night date, Saturday breakfast out, or a shared fifteen minutes or half hour together after work before you meet the demands of dinner. Children and friends will come to respect this sacred time when they learn you're serious about it.

*Honor your differences.* One young wife has discovered that her husband needs time to himself to unwind after a stressful day watching the stock market. They've agreed he'll have a half hour alone before they share the events of the day.

*Share chores.* Housecleaning in tandem gets the job done faster, prevents resentment on the wife's part when he's not doing his share, unites the couple in a common goal, and saves time for more pleasurable pursuits.

*Prevent problems.* See a marriage counselor or sex therapist to improve your communication and handle molehills before they erupt into mountains. Join a couples' therapy group. Sign up for a "Marriage Encounter" weekend (call a church to see if its denomination sponsors one in your area).

*Play together.* Two careers and raising a family—without time for fun—can wear down the best of relationships. How long has it been since you had a water fight while washing the car or watering the yard? A lovemaking session that ended in laughter or a pillow fight?

*Go away alone occasionally.* If you can swing a week's vacation, great. On a smaller scale, aim toward periodic weekend getaways; go out of town or hole up in a downtown hotel room or a comfy bed-and-breakfast inn. Have no money for a sitter—or no grandparents to leave the kids with? Arrange a child-swap with other parents for the night, and stay home to savor the silence. Watch a movie, share a bath, read aloud, dance in the kitchen, make love, sleep in, enjoy breakfast in bed. Then take the host couple's kids so they can enjoy the same.

*Share time with other couples.* We learn more about each other and see our mate in a different light in the company of others. Simplify your calendar and improve your social life by agreeing on a regular dinner (or breakfast or lunch) with friends you both enjoy. Two couples in their forties agreed to have dinner together every Friday night, switching between homes. They enjoyed one another's company (and so did their kids), appreciated the break from having to cook every other weekend, and savored the security of knowing the time together was a given without having to coordinate schedules.

*Develop private rituals and games.* One middle-aged couple plays "piggy toes" with each other's bare feet ("This little piggy went to Paris on vacation..."). Another, in their thirties, reads children's bedtime stories together ("Winnie the Pooh" helps him fall asleep). Another has a signal that means "Let's get rid of the company—I want you!" What are your little games?

Commute together. If you can walk, bus, or drive to work together, you'll gain couple time and perhaps save on gasoline and parking. Some couples enjoy a drink or cup of coffee together after work before heading home.

Time together. That was the original idea, wasn't it?

**KEEP IT SIMPLE: Put your relationship first.**

## MEN: TRY A LITTLE ROMANCE

Michael and Athena Webb celebrated their seventy-fifth wedding anniversary at age twenty-eight.

That's because the Raleigh, North Carolina, couple celebrates each month of marriage.

If that sounds unusual, well, Michael is an unusual guy. Since they began dating in 1989 (they married one and a half years later), he's sent her nearly two hundred cards. He proposed in a huge oak tree that they climbed to lick ice-cream cones while courting.

Not only that, but each Sunday he plays a little game with his wife. He designates a certain place on her as his "kissing spot" and lays a sweet wet one on her there whenever she does something he appreciates—or simply to let her know he loves her.

Sorry, ladies, but this gem of a husband is reserved for a long, long time.

But you can bring a little bit of the Webbs' happy marriage into your home with their bimonthly newsletter, *The RoMANtic: A Practical and Creative Guide to a More Romantic Relationship* (see Resources). Michael is the editor of the newsletter aimed at men.

How did this mere mortal become such a romantic?

The public-relations consultant traces it to a heart-to-heart talk with his mother when he was a teenager.

"My mom came to me with tears in her eyes and sat down. She discussed her two less-than-ideal marriages and the marriages and divorces of my three oldest sisters (I have six sisters and two brothers). My mom pointed to one common problem in all the relationships—emotional neglect. She told me that a woman wants two things from her husband: to be told frequently that she is loved and to be shown frequently that she is special.

"Right then I decided above all, I would be that type of man."

Michael's attentiveness was so noticeable that Athena's friends began asking him to give their boyfriends and husbands some romantic suggestions. He obliged by jotting down some ideas.

When he had more than one hundred, the light bulb for the newsletter blinked on.

Seventy-five percent of the one thousand subscriptions are gifts to men from girlfriends, wives, mothers, sisters, mothers-in-law, and grandmothers. Here's a sampling of Michael's suggestions:

- Don't settle for an average relationship. Remember that your partner needs to be touched, told she's loved, seduced with passion, helped with chores.

- Start a weekend ritual by bringing your mate breakfast in bed. Serve it on a tray with a pretty napkin and a flower.

- Listen for clues as to what your sweetie would love for a gift. Don't give appliances or other impersonal gifts for special occasions.

- Overcome the depression of a rainy day by walking together without an umbrella and stomping in the puddles—or turn off the lights, light some candles, and put on some soft music.

- Pamper your sick sweetie with a get-well basket filled with favorite magazines, the Sunday comics, tea or coffee, fresh fruit, a CD or tape, a rag doll or stuffed animal, etc.

- Trade off years making anniversary plans to surprise the other. The Webbs plan together—and spend a little more—every three years.

- Say "I love you"—or something racier—in a secret code you devise. Cut the letters or numbers out of newspapers and magazines. Mail it, fax it.

- Keep blank cards on hand to mail to her office, tuck into your underwear drawer in thanks for doing the laundry, or put on her car seat.

- Save the flowers your darlin' sends and eventually return them dried in an arrangement, framed under glass, or prepared as a potpourri.

Every relationship can profit from a touch of romance. Among the newsletter subscribers are gay men and lesbians as well as heterosexuals.

"It's all about showing someone you love them and finding a way to express it," Michael says. "Many of us have [love] in our hearts, but we just have a difficult time showing it."

KEEP IT SIMPLE: Put a little romance into each day.

It's natural to focus time and attention on a new love affair. Time together is how we create intimacy.

Now that we're a couple, we may feel that we must socialize only as a couple—and preferably with other couples. There's no longer any room for our single pals when we become a "package deal." And if I don't like my college buddy's wife, this eliminates that couple.

Yet doing all our socializing in couples can restrict the flow of conversation to topics all four people are interested in—not to mention creating jealousies between partners.

Some unhealthy thinking may be responsible for casting friendships aside:

- Our friends are warning us that something's not right, and we don't want to listen.

- Our new sweetheart is unduly possessive. At first we interpret it as a measure of love, but eventually it becomes cloying.

- Our new love doesn't like our old friend, so we give that person up to please him or her. Or perhaps our mate is threatened by the intimacy we share with our friend.

Whatever the case, our friends disappear, and eventually we miss them. It may be hard to strike up those relationships again. But in the long run, it's worth the effort.

In fact, maintaining same-sex friendships may even take some pressure off our marriages.

Here's why:

Anthropologist Helen Fisher, author of *Anatomy of Love*, points out that men and women gain a sense of intimacy in different ways—and for historical reasons.

Women feel intimate by talking face-to-face (perhaps because of the chatting women did with each other as gatherers through the centuries). Men feel intimate through side-by-side doing (aeons of silently tracking animals with other hunters).

This explains why women go out with a friend and spend the time happily gabbing. And guys enjoy a game of handball together or sit in a boat fishing, happily companionable without engaging in "talking things to death." (Yes, there are exceptions to the norm: men who can't shut up and women who don't express their feelings. We're talking predisposition here, not an ironclad rule.)

Instead of insisting that our mates meet all our needs to talk incessantly or sit silently, it makes sense to fulfill some of our needs with same-sex pals. They not only share our needs but understand them.

That's what's meant by not putting all our eggs in one basket.

Spending time with our same-sex friends can give us satisfactions we don't find with our mates. It can give us new perspective and exposure to different experiences. It can give our partners much-needed time alone—and the chance to develop their own good friends.

Fisher makes an interesting point when she says that men and women weren't meant to live cheek-by-jowl. In the early days (and in some present cultures), men spent most of their time with men, and women spent the bulk of their day with other women. In some societies, husbands and wives don't even see each other until it's time to go to bed.

Few of us would be content with a relationship like that. (So what's the point of being married?) But it points out that our culture may put unreasonable emphasis on togetherness.

And what about friends of the opposite sex?

Couples secure in their relationships can allow this. They understand that they can't match all their mate's interests and enthusiasms. And they're up front with each other about the ground rules: their opposite-sex friends are pals, nothing more. Enjoying such friendships while married or partnered requires honesty from all parties.

I know of two couples in their sixties; one of each adored ballroom dancing, but their spouses weren't at all interested. So they found each other—on the dance floor only. Their mates were delighted; it let them off the hook to go dancing, and they didn't have to feel guilty about depriving their partners of such a pleasure.

A secure couple sees friends together and separately, and isn't threatened by the fun one may have with another person. Even separate vacations may indicate partners conscious of their individuality—not a marriage about to fail. Seems to me that being coupled should enrich and broaden our lives, not narrow it.

We may end up calling our mates our best friends. But in the meantime, old friends deserve to be nurtured—even if it's just a phone call or coffee. Friendship is too important to be cast aside.

And sometimes, it even lasts longer than Love of My Life Number Thirty-two.

KEEP IT SIMPLE: Don't give up friends.

# 4. WHATEVER WORKS: CHOICES

*In real love, you want the other person's good. In romantic love, you want the other person.*
—Margaret Anderson

We've come along way from the early television sitcoms in which roles were properly proscribed: Mom at home full time and invariably in the kitchen, Dad heading off each morning from the suburbs to work in the city.

Today, increasing numbers of relationships are built not on pre-set norms but on what works for the couple. Instead of labor division by gender, couples divide chores by who enjoys what—or even trade off to keep the balance fair.

Many Americans survive commuter marriages; other couples choose to stay married yet live apart. Some couples choose separate bedrooms. And thousands enjoy separate vacations.

Today's options allow us to tailor our relationship to fit each partner's needs. We understand that loving one another doesn't mean being in lockstep—or doing things the way our parents did. Too, a loving relationship also gives us leeway to re-adopt some old-fashioned values, flying in the face of modern cultural standards. Women choosing to be at home with small children is an example.

Complex relationships are simplified when we honor differences and choices.

## THE SIMPLE LIFE

Yolanda and Brian McVicker are not like most young couples. Sure, they bought a house, but they're not filling it with wall-sized television screens. They drive a fourteen-year-old car. They don't aspire to hot tubs and fur coats.

This couple—in their thirties—have other things on their agenda. Like having Yolanda at home with their children, Lucy, Samantha, and Kevin. Like living simply without frenzy, emphasizing relationships over possessions. Like enjoying a Sunday dinner together in the dining room, with candles and cloth napkins.

Brian is a firefighter. Yolanda is a full-time mom—with breaks for teaching "Frugal Living" classes three evenings a week through local park and recreation districts. Married since 1982, this sensible couple avoids debt, pays bills monthly, camps or makes day trips for fun, and wears second-hand clothes. It's what they know: She comes from farmer stock, and he is one of twelve kids.

When she was younger, Yolanda wanted sterling, a big house, and a Mercedes. "But as I get older, I see what's really important, and it's not that stuff—it's my family, people I have relationships with," says the petite woman with long dark hair.

Her research shows that before a century ends, Americans typically either spend a lot of money or cut back in favor of a simpler life. And ending a millennium prompts people to spend time reassessing their lives. This may account for the growing "Voluntary Simplicity" movement—and the popularity of Yolanda's classes.

"From what I'm hearing," Yolanda says, "people are tired of the rat race. They're looking at their families and going, 'Time has gone by too fast!'"

While some people falsely interpret simple or frugal living as miserly, the McVickers see this as having a clear idea of where you want to be and what it takes to get there.

Although she worked full time in sales before their marriage, they agreed the trade-off wasn't worth it after deducting all the expenses involved—especially day care. They agree there's a lot to be said for having a mom at home. It's good for their kids and good for them as a couple.

Brian says that when they both worked outside, "We'd come home and nobody wanted to cook. Now we don't have the stress of both of us trying to catch up on home details. We all sit down as a family and have dinner, she does dishes, and I get our son into his bath and his pajamas. Then we still have time to sit down and talk. It's not that panic that other people have."

The McVickers earmark what she makes from teaching for special goals—now it's a computer.

She cans, upholsters, and leads Lucy's 4-H cooking class. He does household repairs, keeps their two cars running, and has even bartered house painting for baby-sitting.

In her "Frugal Living" classes, Yolanda makes these key points:

- Have a budget—no matter how difficult—that both partners keep.

- Don't overbuy. Just because it's on sale or you can afford it doesn't mean you need it.

- Know how much you want to spend when looking for major items.

- Plan weekly menus and "save a ton of money."

- Maintain your car's fluid levels to keep it running smoothly.

- Your child will always know others who have and do what you don't allow yours to have or do. Be strong and say no.

Yolanda and Brian McVicker hope their children will learn to live within their means and put material things in perspective.

Says Yolanda: "Material goods shouldn't rule us—they should be a tool. And things acquired through debt have a tendency to rule us."

Here are some more suggestions to simply family life:

- Decide what's most important to you (such as being home with small children, meals together, family meetings, or weekends together) and weed out the rest.

- Keep a family calendar: Limit evening and weekend activities outside the house. Ink in regular family times.

- Don't overschedule the children; two weekly events (such as Little League and piano lessons) are sufficient.

- If you're trying to pare back and get out of debt, make it a family project. Explain your goals to the kids and enlist their help. (They can't demand advertised toys, they can help conserve electricity and water, and so forth.)

• Turn off the television! Go over the weekly guide and mark a few programs each family member enjoys. Turn the set on only for those shows, then switch it off.

KEEP IT SIMPLE: You—not the television, advertisers, or our consumer culture—must decide what's best for your family.

## FACE IT—WE'RE DIFFERENT

Don't look now, but men and women are different.

In the '70s, we raved that differences existed simply because we raised little boys and girls differently. (Maybe we just hoped it was that easy.)

In the '80s, we did our darnedest to persuade men that they needed to change. We reversed the question, "Why can't a woman be more like a man?" If our man wasn't as easy to talk to as our best girlfriend, we traded him in for a more progressive model. And some of us who found Mr. Sensitive couldn't stand the constant talk about feelings, for Pete's sake!

In the '90s, we concede that men and women are basically different, period. As therapist and author John Gray points out, men don't need to be fixed; the genders just need to understand each other better.

This is progress.

Let's drop that old cutesy, '50s movie notion of the battle-of-the-sexes and instead think of it as confusion-of-the-sexes.

I once heard this confusion explained anthropologically: Men are the way they are (looking for younger, attractive women) because the survival of the species depended in part on him impregnating healthy young females—frequently. Women are attracted to men of power (even if they're not gorgeous specimens) because they required a powerful man's protection for their young—which puts the pictures of a sweet young thing clinging to the arm of old Mr. Moneybags in perspective.

These cave-people arguments sound reasonable—at least for cave-times. As anyone who has mothered knows, instinct is very much with us. We're not so far from our primitive origins as we'd like to think.

Instead of male- or female-bashing and endlessly trying to fix each other, let's keep the old cave in mind—and unleash our sense of humor—as we attempt to deal with pet peeves between the sexes:

*Why doesn't he/she understand?* Why do you think we call it the opposite sex? Find a same-sex friend to talk to. It saves frustration and translation time.

*She doesn't want a solution, she just wants to complain.* Hey, sometimes we just need to hear "poor baby" before we can get around to solutions. We can ask—or tell—what's needed at the moment.

*Why doesn't he put the lid down/why doesn't she leave it up?* Ah, the never-ending question. Try putting a life jacket next to the potty to make your point.

*Why does he watch so much television sports?* My first husband couldn't tear his eyes off the tube—football, I think it was. So I stripped down, donned the kids' cowboy hat and holsters, and stood in front of the television. He merely motioned me to move out of the way. Note that I said *"first* husband."

*Why doesn't he enjoy shopping as much as I do?* Face it: Men have the uncanny knack of dashing into a store and buying the first shirt they see. On the other hand, they can kill an afternoon in a car-parts/hardware/sporting-goods store. Solution: Don't go shopping with each other. If you do, try what works with the kids: If he doesn't whine, you'll buy him an ice-cream cone when you're finished. Try to enjoy the fact that your life is a "Cathy" cartoon.

*Why do we have the same old argument?* Spare yourselves monotony and switch roles! You already know each other's lines, right? This may give you a fresh perspective—or you'll get to laughing so hard it'll be hard to fight.

*Why doesn't he do his share of the chores?* If CONDEMNED signs slapped around the house don't work, write "Daddy, please give me a bath" on a Post-it and stick it on the kid. If all else fails, both of you can chip in to hire help.

*Honey, I'm just not in the mood.* OK, men aren't always ready—no matter what Mom warned—and women are often too pooped to pucker up. Let's compromise: Whoever is in the mood gives the other five dollars to give it a go. (Either of you would wait five minutes for a bus, wouldn't you?) When the bucks add up, go out for a romantic dinner together.

Even as we try to understand how the other gender works, we'll continue to have pet peeves. Let's keep it in perspective, though.

Our lives can change forever with one phone call, one knock on the door. And then we'd give anything to have our partner back, lid up or down.

**KEEP IT SIMPLE: Love is more important than the frustrations it causes.**

## REDEFINING ROLES

Remember how it goes, according to the old movies and early television reruns? You grow up and get married. She keeps house and raises children; he goes off to work—and doesn't do the laundry when he gets home, thank you.

The roles of conjugal partners used to be clearly defined; husband and wife each knew what was expected.

Times are changing.

Some people love each other but can't or don't marry. Some decide not to have children. Some multiple-married folks couldn't rack up a silver anniversary even if they added all their I-do's together. And some couples change most of the rules. Their lives cancel out years of Donna Reed reruns.

Five courageous women (who prefer to remain anonymous) shared their choices during a women's retreat. Here are the situations:

*Living together.* This thirty-nine-year-old has lived with her male partner for twelve years. They don't plan to marry or to have children. They love each other but enjoy their differences and try to avoid the "we-ness" they find cloying (as in "We love that restaurant"). They take separate vacations; she enjoys European jaunts with women friends while "he thinks going to the river is a big trip." She bought the house; he does the repairs. They have separate bank accounts and a list of what they own together. Her family doesn't understand, "but then family approval is not at the top of my list."

*Longtime married.* This forty-four-year-old married nearly twenty-nine years ago, with all the odds against her: she was a fifteen-year-old pregnant bride. The couple had two more children and played fairly traditional roles, "until I decided money was power, and it was real important to me to make my own." Best friends since they met, they're also committed to close friends. She calls marriage "a twenty-nine-year workshop" that they may not always have. But today they choose it and delight in it. "We went into it for the long run, but there's no assurance this relationship will go on another five years or six months. And that's freeing; it adds another element of choice."

*Lesbian partnership.* This twenty-nine-year-old has been involved with other women for eight years—and jokes she can't find a

Valentine's Day card for her situation. She knows she's lucky: her parents consider her partner their daughter-in-law. She describes her life as "having woman-energy every day." Chores are assigned as to who has experience and who likes to do what (she cooks, her partner does dishes). "Society teaches that women are weak and you should be scared with another woman, but the lawn still gets mowed and the oil gets changed. It's not great when you have PMS at the same time, but she knows how you feel!"

*Married but apart.* This forty-eight-year-old has been married twenty-eight years, but three years ago her husband was transferred out of state, and she stayed to work and keep the kids in school. "I kept saying I was going to join him in a few months, but I didn't want to leave my job and support system. I told him—and asked if the marriage was over. He understood and was totally supportive." Their mothers and co-workers thought it odd, but periodic weekends together worked. The marriage has weathered a miscarriage, bankruptcy, alcohol problems, and counseling, and now a new test looms: he's been transferred home.

*Single.* This forty-seven-year-old was married fourteen years, then single fourteen more. She and her husband separated for six months and then got back together for a year. "It was our happiest, but I'd gotten used to being on my own—and seeing how other men treated me," so they divorced. She had several relationships ranging from one to four years but has had none for the past two years. "I faced the fear of being alone, and I love it. I'm giving myself permission to see what happens." With a friend who was devastated when her marriage of twenty-five years ended, she went to law school and is now considering switching from a fourth-grade classroom to a courtroom.

Which option is best? None will speak for anyone but herself. These women just know that their relationship choices suit them and their partners for now.

Does yours?

**KEEP IT SIMPLE: Your relationship needs to work for the two of you, nobody else.**

## CHILD-FREE BY CHOICE OR CHANCE

It's an overcast Saturday morning, and the day yawns leisurely ahead for Kelly and Chris Swinford.

He's up early, listening to music; she sleeps in. Then they're off to breakfast at their favorite restaurant. Back at their tidy, two-bedroom apartment, she works on her ceramics hobby until they decide to skip off to a nearby river to hunt for pretty rocks.

Their evening also hinges on whim. Maybe they'll go out for dinner; perhaps they'll stay in.

The Swinfords, in their thirties, call the shots freely because they don't have children. And that's how they plan to keep it. It's not that they don't like kids. Eventually, they plan to do volunteer work with them. It's just that Chris, the oldest of three siblings, realizes she doesn't have the patience to parent. Kelly, who has a younger sister, never wanted kids.

When they married in 1983, they decided to wait five years before considering the baby question. "Then we discussed it for a year, and decided it just wasn't for us," says Chris, a strawberry blonde with big glasses.

Instead, the couple has cats: Nermal, an orange tiger, and D.C., a fat cat who waddles. ("D.C. want food? Follow Daddy," Chris directs.) And plants. And hobby materials left out undisturbed on the kitchen table. And a "room of doom" with small-electronics stuff and records and tapes in orderly piles.

She's a receptionist and college student studying graphic design; he's an electronics technician doing volcano and landslide research.

As firstborns, Kelly and Chris aren't unusual. Studies show that firstborn children are less likely to become parents. They cite these reasons: They've already had too much responsibility taking care of younger siblings. They've seen the downside of parenting as their folks struggled with younger siblings. They want to develop themselves instead of caring for others.

Whatever the birth order of the spouses, child-free households make up the majority of American homes. According to the U.S. Census Bureau, 53 percent are either married without children under eighteen, or single without children (52 million in 1992 versus 42.5 million in 1980).

Precise statistics are hard to come by. But the percentage of women who have never had children appears to be rising. In 1976, 10.2 percent of all women forty to forty-four had never borne a child. By 1992, the figure had risen to 16 percent.

The Swinfords joined the 2,500-member Childfree Network, a support and educational group, so they wouldn't feel alone in a world of baby boomers having babies. Network members also lobby for their rights. They resent tax breaks for kids, references to family values that imply they aren't a family, laws that prevent people under fifty-five from having child-free neighborhoods, and the lack of child-free seating in planes and restaurants.

Leslie Lafayette, a former high-school teacher in Citrus Heights, California, operated the network from 1992 to 1997. The butterfly was the symbol for the Childfree Network, which stressed "child-free" over "childless" because the latter suggests a lack. Lafayette advocates better parenting education beginning at twelve. She wants the media to reflect the difficulty of parenting. And she wants people to "feel freer about not having children." Parenthood, she emphasizes, should be by choice—not chance. Childless by Choice is a similar support group (see Resources).

Some of the group's members are infertile and accept it; others just don't want children; some simply never got around to having kids. "If we want to do anything, buy anything, go anywhere, we can do it anytime," says Kelly. "We don't have to look for some-body to take care of the kids, pack the car up, or plan. It's that freedom we enjoy."

The way the Swinfords see it, they're helping the Earth: "The planet's overpopulated as it is, and it's going to get worse," says Chris. The Swinfords contend they won't regret their decision in old age because they know themselves so well.

To those considering whether to become parents, Kelly says, "No matter what your parents or other people think, you're the ones who have to live with the decision. Realize it's a choice. And if you don't have kids, there are people and an organization you can talk to. We're here."

**KEEP IT SIMPLE: Honor your own choices.**

## DIFFERING SPIRITUAL PATHS

Carole has been on a spiritual path since she was a teenager, when she led her family to attending church.

She dreamed of marrying a man embarked on the same quest, a man who'd enjoy her church, talking with like-minded people, and, as she puts it, "pondering the universe."

Carole thought she'd found this questing quality in Kirk, the son of a minister. The brief romance showed her that "he put on a spiritual act to impress women—he talked the talk but didn't walk the walk."

Then she met and married Vince, a fallen-away Catholic whose idea of spirituality is weekends in the woods at their cabin.

She took him to church; he had trouble keeping his face straight. "It's like a television parody—a convention of Kirks," says Vince. "It feels shallow to me—with nothing churchlike about it."

Now in their thirties and happily married five years, the couple has made many adjustments and accommodations. Following divergent spiritual paths is one of them.

Can a marriage survive such differences?

Yes, say Vince and Carole—and experts such as Susan Jeffers, best-selling author of the books *Feel the Fear and Do It Anyway*, *Opening Our Hearts to Men*, and *End the Struggle and Dance with Life*. But survival requires mutual respect and love.

"If both [individuals] are loving toward one another and each allows the other's growth, yes," Jeffers says. "It involves both being strong and enlightened for that to happen. It isn't necessary for both to be doing the same thing."

But we don't always realize that.

"In the beginning, we get too far into superiority. 'I'm doing the spiritual path and you're just stuck'—which is the worst thing one can do," she continues. "One looks down at the other. And the other partner gets defensive and threatened. When one's judgmental, it's not a very spiritual stance to take.

"The ultimate in spiritual growth is love—and often people on a spiritual path are unloving to people who aren't doing the same thing they're doing." Carole concedes she was disappointed in Vince's attitude at first. "It took me four years together to realize he's never going to be this spiritual guy."

They say their adjustment process went through several stages: recognizing the differences, feeling disappointed, coping, and respecting each other's right to be different.

"Spirituality is about searching for our safety zone, feeling safe and loved—and we realized we go about it in different ways," Vince says. She goes to church with a friend and enjoys discussing the lesson, while he jumps on his motorcycle and savors the wind in his face.

When one partner embarks on a spiritual path well into a relationship, the process can be as difficult as making any change—such as returning to school or work. Jeffers says the key is for the changing person to understand that his or her partner may feel threatened.

Jeffers's first marriage broke up when she was thirty-four and wanted to go back to school after the children were born. "I was immature, and I put him down instead of helping him cope. I got very righteous."

Carole realizes now that she is not being fair in asking Vince to meet all of her needs and that it's more important that they share the same basic values and morals. When the kids come along, they agree they want them to attend church—probably her choice of denomination since she would be the most motivated to take them.

As Jeffers says, "We must realize everyone has their own path—and it's not necessarily yours."

**KEEP IT SIMPLE: True spirituality puts love first.**

## COPING WITH A COMMUTER MARRIAGE

This is a story about a father and mother working together—even though they were 165 miles apart most of the past two years.

Meet Cheryl and Greg Conrad, in their thirties, and their carrot-top kids, Ryan and Megan.

From September 1994 to May 1996, Cheryl burned rubber each week—except summers and school breaks—between her home in suburban Portland, Oregon, and the University of Puget Sound campus in Tacoma, Washington. As a result of commitment and compromise, she graduated from the university's two-year occupational-therapy program and works with disabled people, helping them function and live more satisfactorily.

The plan worked because this couple set priorities—a tenet of simplicity.

For eighteen months, Cheryl followed a routine: School all week, with time-outs for a 7 P.M. phone call home and some laps around the school track. At noon each Friday after class, hop in the car for the two-and-one-half-hour drive home. Play with the kids and husband, hole up to study, and spend all Sunday as a family. Then be off by 6 A.M. Monday and north on I-5 in time for class.

"You don't totally appreciate what your wife does until she's gone. I realized what a good wife and mother she is," says Greg, a pharmacist.

The Conrads were high-school sweethearts. They married a year after Cheryl graduated, and she worked as a medical transcriptionist to put him through school. When Megan was eighteen months old, Cheryl started community-college night classes, earning two associate degrees. She wanted to become an occupational therapist.

Turned down by a program closer to home, Cheryl applied at Puget Sound. When she was accepted so far from home, "I thought, 'Oh no,' and cried. But I wanted so badly to go." Greg said, "Go."

"The kids were our foremost concern," he says. "We have a very strong marriage, so we knew it would survive." Stability, they say, was the key. Cheryl never left on Sunday, no matter how early she had to be in class Monday. Ritual and routine helped the arrangement work.

Each Monday, Megan and Ryan found comics from Mom in their lunches. They also found a continuing story she wrote for them each week—a two-year saga featuring the children. A weekly calendar enabled the children to check off the days, and at the end of each semester, they celebrated with build-your-own sundaes. Every other weekend, each child enjoyed the treat of time alone with Mom. They toured the Tacoma campus and the home she shared with another student. With a copy of her daily schedule, it was easy for the kids to visualize just where Mom was and what she was doing every minute of the day.

During breaks and summers, Cheryl cooked and froze dinners for her family. The Conrad freezer has held up to one hundred labeled, mom-to-microwave meals.

"People razzed me about it, but it meant less stress for Greg. I didn't want my family at McDonald's every night. My goal was to do this with the least amount of stress for the family."

"Cheryl has incredible organizational skills," boasts Greg, who had a stringent schedule himself. Friends helped out: pals who took over if a child was sick, buddies who rotated picking up the children from school, snow-day friends.

The two-year disruption was a family investment, the Conrads say. After Cheryl works to pay off her $30,000 in school loans, her part-time salary will go toward their retirement.

"It's made our marriage more fifty-fifty," Cheryl says. "Not that it has to be equal, but we share more what needs to be done now. Greg's even more emotionally there for the kids."

To others considering a commuter marriage, the Conrads urge paring debt before the change. Sacrifice to pay phone bills in order to stay in touch daily. Be organized so the kids have predictability.

"I bonded with the kids like I never would have before," Greg says. "The kids got some independence—and a better father in the end."

And young Ryan is still grinning about graduation. "The most exciting part was when they called Mom's name. It was like we'd accomplished something very big—something we all accomplished together."

**KEEP IT SIMPLE:** Working together helps you weather any situation.

## WORKAHOLISM KILLS RELATIONSHIPS

Set your work aside for a second and take a quiz:

When you sit and do nothing, do you feel guilty or anxious? Do family members complain about how much you work? Do you feel uncomfortable if you're not busy? Do you prefer to help organize events in order to avoid sitting around and talking to people?

If you're answering yes, you may have a problem with workaholism. And you needn't be a high-powered executive to qualify: homemakers, volunteers, students, retirees, hobbyists, employees, and bosses all can suffer.

The key is whether or not you use activity to distract yourself from your feelings, from intimacy with yourself and others. Workaholism isn't about productivity; it's about staying busy.

Have you ever been so busy arranging a funeral that you didn't feel the pain until afterward? Most people use activity at some point to avoid dealing with feelings.

Overworking is a serious compulsion that can destroy marriages and even cause death. And it doesn't lead to a simpler life.

While the number of workaholics is unknown, the American work week has increased from forty hours to 43.2. People work longer hours today than ever before in this century. The American Medical Association acknowledged in the April 1990 *Journal* that work stress and heart attacks are related.

What's the difference between a hard worker and a workaholic?

The hard worker is busy with a project, enjoys it, and returns to other aspects of life when the work is done. Just because you work hard and feel passionate about your job doesn't mean you're a workaholic. Hard workers take care of themselves and maintain balance in their lives; they make changes if they get stressed.

Workaholics, on the other hand, have no limits. They don't necessarily enjoy what they're doing. They work like automatons. And they persist with the frantic activity even when it affects them adversely (poor health, spouse and children suffering, etc.).

Despite the fact that work addiction is applauded by employers and society, it carries high personal costs:

- Unable to pace themselves, workaholics burn out and get sick.

- Workaholics are unavailable to their families, physically and emotionally; the chance of divorce is high.

- Spouses may feel so neglected they begin an extramarital affair.

- Teenage children of workaholics often turn to alcohol and other drugs to ease the pain resulting from no emotional connection to that parent. The kids may have material things, but they long for time with the parent.

Again, the individual's frantic pace characterizes workaholism. Even a vacation may be hectic, as the busy-addict continues to run from self and others through constant activity.

What's the solution?

Learn more about Workaholics Anonymous, a free twelve-step support group based on the tenets of Alcoholics Anonymous. Reading books about compulsive behavior may help. Spouses of workaholics may be helped by attending Al-Anon meetings to learn how to focus on themselves instead of on the addicted person.

**KEEP IT SIMPLE: People matter more than work.**

## CHEATING HEARTS OOZE EXCUSES

Amazing, the range of excuses we come up with when we stray. They aren't even original:

*We didn't plan this; it just happened.* We may not seek an affair, but we do have some control when things begin to heat up. Feeling strong attraction for someone else isn't a sin. But rationalizing little meetings, lunches, or drinks after work may be leading up to one.

*We were drunk; we weren't responsible.* Let's be honest! Chances are we put ourselves in harm's way while sober: we huddled in a bar while claiming to work late, visited a friend's husband while she's out of town, etc.

*His wife doesn't understand him/They fight all the time/He only stays with her because she's pregnant.* God's gotta flinch each time she hears one of these! Remember this cliché instead: The person who lies to a spouse will lie to you. (And she got pregnant all by herself?)

*We're not hurting anyone as long as we're discreet.* It's easy to think that people won't be hurt if they don't find out—but don't count on that. In the meantime, we're robbing our spouses and the kids of our time, attention, and energy.

And why do we have illicit affairs?

We're lonely, and we're flattered by someone's attention. We don't think we deserve a person all our own. We're willing to settle for less. We think we're impervious to being caught. We're rationalizing. We don't give a damn about others. We're still trying to win Mom or Dad away from the other parent. We're incredibly naive. Or maybe we're sleazeballs.

Oh yes, that other reason: a lover is incredibly more exciting than what I—or my lover—have at home. All that great sex, high romance, and no responsibility! How exciting would it be if the affair ended and the work of sustaining a day-to-day relationship began? Not very.

Now, I don't think a "homewrecker" comes along and ruins a happy marriage or perfect partnership. But we do weight the odds when we take up with a married person or have an extramarital affair ourselves. We have only so much time and energy. If we spent just half the time on a partner that we do on a lover, the relationship would have to improve.

Too, we have no idea at the time of the eventual price we'll pay. We have to live with our guilt—and be reminded of it daily—whether we stay with our partner or take up with the new one. We may have the agony of confronting a lover's spouse or kids. Or even our own.

When my father left my mother for a woman younger than I was, I saw—up close and raw—the devastation such impulses wreak on a wife, children, and even grandchildren and in-laws. Seeing the pain on my mother's face that I could have put on some other woman's is cruel karma indeed.

Perhaps illicit affairs are more than impractical. Perhaps they are just plain wrong.

If infidelity tempts you or has affected your marriage, consider these points:

- **Adultery doesn't mean the end of the marriage; the union can survive and gain strength. But this takes work and time. The transgressing party must earn back a partner's trust.**

- Honesty, openness, and understanding are crucial to rebuilding the relationship, which some experts say takes about two years.

- Counseling, a couples' support group, and reading about adultery can help.

- Children are affected by adultery more than their parents can know.

- Partners should acknowledge their attraction to others. If we can talk about it, we're less likely to act on it.

- If you're having an affair, end it and commit to your marriage. No fair trying to hang on to one relationship in case the other doesn't work out.

As Mom used to say, "Everything has its price." Sometimes, the price is just too great.

**KEEP IT SIMPLE: Don't cheat.**

## HIM, HER, AND THE WHEELCHAIR

Fifteen-year-old Wanda and eighteen-year-old Ray stood before the Presbyterian minister and repeated the familiar words.

Wanda had dropped out of high school to marry the boy she'd adored since age eleven. She'd persuaded her mom to let her do the shopping at his parents' San Diego grocery just so she could see that cute Ray—who regarded her as a pesky little flirt. Later, Wanda haunted the beach where he was a part-time lifeguard; suddenly she didn't seem so young.

Although she was pregnant and everyone predicted the marriage wouldn't last, it did—through Ray's rise from bottle boy to grocery manager, the birth of three kids, a move to the Pacific Northwest.

Then, another test of their relationship: The couple was rushing a sick friend to the emergency room when fate's fist—a drunken driver—smashed into their car. At age twenty-nine, Ray became a quadriplegic. At age twenty-six, Wanda traded the role of wife for caretaker. Debbie was ten, Ray was nine, and Karen was seven.

He'll be a vegetable, people said. Put him in a nursing home, people said. Get a job to support your kids, people said. Ray and Wanda Morris told them no.

Instead of the predicted year in the hospital, Ray exercised his way out in six months. He regained some motion of his left shoulder and enough in his right to feed himself, sign his name, and even bowl.

"I just couldn't put him in a nursing home," Wanda says simply. "I never wanted a divorce, or even thought of it. It wasn't an option." Nor would she leave home to work; Ray and the kids needed her more than ever. She baby-sat for extra money.

The marriage was decidedly different. Ray missed being able to get down on the floor and scuffle with his kids—and later, his grandkids. Wanda ached just to be held by Ray. "Before the accident, we always slept in each other's arms, and now he couldn't hold me. That's what I miss."

They came to realize that marriage is not based on honeymoon sex.

For fourteen years, Wanda managed by herself, lifting Ray, bathing him, tending to his bathroom needs. When he developed pressure sores, she blamed herself. By this time, her evening glasses of wine had gotten out of control.

"Please stop drinking," Ray begged.

"Don't tell me what to do!" she snapped. She went to stay with her mother, sobered up, came home, and relapsed again. Finally, she entered alcoholism treatment; she's been sober three years.

"Wanda hung with me through the accident," says Ray. "Now she had a disease and it was my turn to help her through hers." Sobriety and couples' counseling helped the Morrises over this hurdle. Now they're passing on what they've learned the hard way. They lead a monthly support group, "Mobility Impaired and Families," at a local hospital.

Today, Ray and Wanda know that one caretaker can't handle everything, that the unimpaired partner has to have time alone. They've learned that listening to one's own feelings—and to the other's—is essential. They know that true marriage means not giving up on the other. Ever.

Going into their thirty-seventh year of marriage, the couple enjoys bowling, garage sales, and walking the dogs (with Ray in his motorized wheelchair). They go to dinner once a week, rent funny videos, and baby-sit the grandkids. He admires her fortitude, her sense of humor, her giving nature. She applauds his lack of anger, his acceptance, his easygoing temperament.

Will the Morrises make it through to the last part of the promise they made so long ago? "Looks that way," says Ray. "We've had our ups and downs, but we've made it through it all."

"You just have to accept life on life's terms," says Wanda. "You have to make the best of what you have."

**KEEP IT SIMPLE: Remember that love is a promise.**

## WOUNDING WITH WORDS

"Sticks and stones may break my bones, but names will never hurt me." That childhood taunt was intended to make us feel better. It didn't really work, but then lies usually don't.

Names and ugly words hurt. They wound us deeply, whether they come from lovers, parents, teachers, bosses, or friends.

Such conversational ugliness is verbal abuse. And like other forms of abuse, it leaves scars. One author calls verbal abusers "psychological terrorists."

Verbal abuse is most damaging when we are children, because children believe what their parents say. Told often enough that we are stupid, irresponsible, lazy, or awkward, we gradually accept this as the truth.

In adulthood, we play the same tape, telling ourselves, "Of course I can't do my taxes—I'm stupid at math" or "I can't hope for a promotion—I couldn't handle the responsibility" or "I'm too lazy to be a really good housekeeper."

The poison darts of verbal abuse take many forms:

*Yelling.* "Damn it, I'm talking to you!" Abusers who scream often say they are doing it to get our attention.

*Name-calling.* "Hey stupid! You're so lazy and selfish." These people often use ugly racist and sexist terms as well.

*Teasing.* "Gain any more weight, and the kids will confuse you with Santa." This is the only way some people know how to relate. But if the recipient and others aren't laughing, the taunt's not funny.

*Sarcasm.* "Of all the people I could have married, I drew the short stick and got you." This is often followed by "I was just teasing—can't you take a joke?" Psychologist DeLoss "Dee" Friesen calls sarcasm "hit-and-run put-downs."

*Put-downs.* "What makes you think you could get a job?" Some people put others down to put themselves up (to feel superior).

*Invalidating.* "You have no reason to feel that way." This repudiates the other's feelings, which no one has the right to do.

*Criticizing.* "Why isn't this B an A?" These comments are often justified as "helping you do better," but they make the accused feel worse.

*Sexual innuendo.* "I love it when we get to work late together." This can be very threatening to the other person, who may feel uncomfortable without knowing why.

*Not talking.* Withholding conversation can be just as punishing as any of the above.

Because verbal abuse is often subtle—and you may have grown used to it—it may be difficult to identify. Here are some clues: You feel confused, unheard, manipulated, hurt, angry—and just plain yucky. You want to get away, end the conversation, lash out, defend yourself. You may explain yourself to death, cry, doubt your own feelings, shut up entirely and continue to drag your resentments around, or busy yourself analyzing and/or excusing why your abuser is behaving this way.

Friesen finds that verbal abusers won't acknowledge the abuse: They claim instead that you caused it, it didn't happen, or it's really not so bad. That leaves you to set limits: "I don't allow people to talk to me that way." "I care about you and this relationship, but I won't take this. You'll have to stop or I'll have to leave." "This feels abusive; I'm going to end this conversation now."

Sound scary? It is. Standing up against verbal abuse requires healthy self-esteem and firm personal boundaries.

How to get them? Support groups and being around support-ive people will increase your confidence. A good therapist can help, as can reading books about self-esteem, assertiveness, and codependency.

Doing nothing can lead to physical abuse and cause the relationship to deteriorate even further. Doing nothing tells your partner you'll take whatever that person dishes out. You deserve better.

This list is used at support meetings to help people in abusive situations:

## PERSONAL BILL OF RIGHTS

1. Your life has choices beyond mere survival.

2. You have a right to say no to anything when you feel you are not ready or feel unsafe.

3. Life is not motivated by fear.

4. You have a right to all your feelings.

5. You are probably not guilty.

6. You have a right to make mistakes.

7. There is no need to smile when you cry.

8. You have a right to end conversations in which you feel humiliated and put down.

9. You can be emotionally healthier than the people around you.

10. It is OK to be relaxed, playful, and frivolous.

11. You have a right to change and grow.

12. It is important to set limits and be selfish.

13. You can be angry at someone you love.

14. It is OK to take care of yourself.

**KEEP IT SIMPLE: Abuse is never OK.**

## WHEN RELIGIONS CONFLICT

Pete and Donna Kaufman met in a college psychology class.

"I guess it was Freudian, in a way," Pete says with a laugh.

An understanding of what makes people work came in handy for the Cincinnati couple, now married two decades and the parents of three children.

Pete is Jewish and Donna is Catholic. They know the pressures that interfaith couples face. And so they started *Crosswinds: The Newsletter about Interfaith Relationships*, a compendium of problems, solutions, book reviews, statistics, and commentary on the growing phenomenon of couples from different religions (see Resources).

The Kaufmans say they're not advocating interfaith unions, just acknowledging them.

About 33 million American adults live in households in which at least one adult has a different religious identification, researchers Barry Kosmin and Seymour Lachman note in *One Nation under God*.

Interfaith marriages are increasing. In 1957, the proportion of U.S. residents who married within their denomination was 94 percent for Jews, 88 percent for Catholics, 83 percent for Baptists, and about 81 percent for Lutherans, Methodists, and Presbyterians.

Forty years later, we read a different story. An estimated 40 to 50 percent of Americans marry outside their faith. Studying more than 113,000 people, the researchers discovered that 22 percent of Catholics—6.5 million—live with someone of a different religion. And half of Jews now marry outside their faith.

"We had a long, arduous struggle to come to some decisions ourselves, and we thought there was a need for a newsletter," Pete says. "We know there are hundreds of thousands of couples like us, and no one gives them much support. Couples need to know they're not the only ones."

*Crosswinds* debuted in December 1995, with the majority of subscribers in Jewish/Christian marriages. Readers run the gamut, though, from Methodists married to Hindus to Episcopalians joined to Buddhists.

Interfaith couples face many hurdles, including disapproving parents and extended family and clergy who predict it won't work. (A priest told Donna she'd burn in hell.) Also, it can be difficult to accept and respect the partner's religious beliefs and traditions, celebrate holidays, and raise children.

The Kaufmans' children are Jewish, but they know that Mama has a Christmas tree, and they've accompanied her to Mass. They've attended the first communions of their cousins and a bat mitzvah. "They are getting an interesting education in how the world really works," says their dad. "And that's not necessarily bad."

The Kaufmans—she's the newsletter's publisher, he's editor, and both maintain regular jobs—contend that intermarriage makes couples stronger as they learn what is truly important to them as individuals and as a pair. "We want people to know that it's OK to be married to somebody of a different faith," Pete says. "The world is not going to stop spinning on its axis.

"Love may not necessarily conquer all, but with communication it can triumph."


KEEP IT SIMPLE: Respect your differences.

Cliff and Regina Ellis stand at the front of the church, his arm tenderly about her waist. Before the gathering of family and friends, the young couple lights five white candles. They share a kiss that puts a catch in the throats of onlookers.

Is this their wedding? They certainly are demonstrating their commitment.

But no. This is a memorial service for their five-year-old daughter, Alexandra, who had battled cancer for two years.

The day before she died, her parents helped her out of this world just as they'd welcomed her into it—by getting into the bathtub and cuddling her close in the warm, safe water.

They spoke to her of dolphins, just like the one she'd swum with in Hawaii weeks before. They tucked her into their big bed in a quiet upstairs room, lit candles, played soft music, sang her favorite songs quietly, and held her close. She said goodbye to her kitten, Simba, her three-year-old brother, Zachary, and five generations of family and friends. When she stopped breathing, they spent several more hours with their firstborn, then let her go.

Only thirty-one and twenty-nine years old, Cliff and Regina are an unusual young couple. Strong. Loving. Wise beyond their years. While a child's terminal illness stresses a marriage terribly, Alex's long fight and death has further cemented theirs.

Reflecting on their daughter's death and its effects two months later, they decide that this cement is commitment: commitment to each other, to being the parents Zach deserves, to the foundation they've established to provide information and support to other children with cancer. And commitment to hanging in there for this terrible, topsy-turvy year, which one moment finds them appreciating the sunset and the next wondering how life can be so cruel.

Regina Rathburn and Cliff Ellis met in high school in the early '80s, she a freshman and he a senior. They dated off and on, getting serious in her senior year.

They seemed to be soul mates, clicking with each other as they did with no one else. Cliff was "funny, sensitive, warm"; Regina was "beautiful, with a really strong personality. We really connected."

In 1987, they got engaged, and she spent the summer studying in Italy: "A time of independence and awareness of my strength. It prepared me for what lay ahead."

Cliff's dad died, forcing him to drop out of college, take over the family business, and pay the mortgage for his mother and handicapped sister.

When they married in 1988, they wanted several children—the kind of family that Regina knew, where people talk things out, laugh and cry together. "I was always realistic," Regina says. "I knew marriage took a lot of hard work. I never had the expectation it'd be sweet and wonderful. If we were going to grow and change, it'd be hard work."

Alexandra was born soon after. At first she was a perfect baby, but she developed breathing problems. When she finally came home, they climbed into a warm bathtub with their daughter, safe in fate's hands.

Three years later, Zach joined their household. Their dreams were coming true, and they had plenty of time for their children as they managed their business.

Then Alex was diagnosed with cancer on her spine. For two and one-half years, they fought the good fight, complete with chemotherapy. Cliff shaved his head to match his bald daughter's "chemo cut."

Late in the winter, the cancer came back. Alex declined a bone-marrow transplant; no more hospitals, she begged. She wanted to go to Hawaii and swim with a dolphin. So they did.

Neither parent knew how the other would react when the end came. Would they still be the same people? Could they even love each other after such a loss?

Yet as she lay dying in her parents' big bed, Alexandra gave them a gift: "She took our hands over the top of her and created this bond," says her mother. "I looked at Cliff, and thought, 'God, he's so beautiful!' What a father! I saw in him this love, this incredible giving. We were there for her 100 percent—teamwork. We honored our hearts, our daughter, our relationship—just like we did with her birth."

Cliff's and Regina's eyes lock across their living room as they recall that unforgettable night. "And I looked at Regina and couldn't imagine loving her more. I was drawn even closer to her—unbelievable."

Here's what keeps them together:

- They know that grief is a solitary act, and they give each other space.

- They understand that marriage—especially one under stress—has its ups and downs. Some days are simply down days and not a reason to leave.

- They agree that children are their first job—and their first joy. Procrastinate on anything, but make time for your children, they urge other parents.

- They have knowledge—hard-won and unusual for people so young—that life is short and to be savored. They spend their limited time only with people—or at activities—they enjoy and find meaningful.

- They appreciate that time changes people, and they encourage each other to grow.

- They acknowledge that even in the bleakest time, there are gifts to be discovered.

"I thought Alex's death was going to ravage us—that losing her would be losing myself," admits Regina. "I didn't know who I was anymore, but Cliff said, 'Whoever we are, we'll be together.'"

**KEEP IT SIMPLE: Know that united, you can cope.**

# 5. COMING UNDONE: SEPARATION AND DIVORCE

'Tis better to have loved and lost
Than never to have loved at all.
—Alfred Lord Tennyson

It's not easy to stay up when love gets you down. And glorious as love is, it will get you down.

She moves out while you're at work. He cancels everything a month before the wedding. She honeys up over the phone one night and sounds aloof the next. He asks for a divorce out of the blue.

What's going on here? Sometimes it's hard to tell. That's why we have so many love songs, not to mention country songs. (Do you know what happens when you play a country-music record backwards? Your lover comes back, and so does your dog.)

Love never seems to get easier. No matter how old we are, it's still high school—with no prom to look forward to. "I'm too old for all this!" you tell a friend, slightly embarrassed at chronicling your latest breakup.

Breaking up—at any age—just plain hurts. Whether it's from a three-month romance, a years-long "understanding," or a long-term marriage, we can expect to go through a period of grieving. How we handle it depends on the circumstances of the breakup and whether we were the one who left or got left, the investment of time, the complications (packing up the television is easier than carting off the kids), and the degree of acrimony involved.

Most of all, how we cope depends on our outlook. Do we blame our ex for everything, feel like a victim, and moan that we'll never love or be loved again? Or can we treasure the good times, own up to our part of what went wrong, and wish our former love well?

During this difficult time, we need to simplify more than ever, to lighten our load, not only physically but emotionally.

Breaking up hurts, but you can survive. And chances are good you'll live to love again.

## HAPPILY EVER AFTER?

He leans over the expensive dessert and slides the engagement ring onto her finger. The candlelight reflects in their eyes, mirroring their hopes of happiness ever after.

*He sits on the edge of his seat; she dabs at her eyes. The marriage counselor leans back in his padded chair, his fingertips shaping a pyramid. The words are nearly as old as the shape he creates: "He doesn't talk to me." "We have nothing in common." "All he cares about is work." "All she cares about is the kids."*

The months before the wedding are a frantic flurry of florists, caterers, gowns, and gift registers. Sure, they bicker some; every time he asks, "What's it matter what I wear?" she wants to slug him. It's a lot of work—and money—creating the most perfect day of their lives. But it will be perfect.

*The clock in the hallway strikes midnight as she thumbs through the television section in search of an old movie, a rerun, anything to justify delaying bed a while longer. Bedtime has become a contest of wills: He stays awake, she sits up watching television. Anything to avoid the reproachful, convoluted conversations, the pleas to be held, the accidental touching of feet that triggers a torrent of tears.*

She tugs the tissue off yet another chip-and-dip set at her second shower in a week and blinks back happy tears. All these women lavishing love on her: her mom and soon-to-be mother-in-law, her sis, the girls she's known from grade school. What fun it is to be a bride!

*The man at the door is wearing a sheriff's uniform. He turns over the paper she's been expecting; she's been "served." Her husband has filed for divorce. She's ice-cube cool until she begins to read the legal jargon that reduces her dreams to "whereas" and "heretofore." But* worst of all, their children—their darling, precious children—are referred to as "the legal issue of this marriage." One hanky won't sop up the ensuing sobs.

The church looks as perfect as they'd planned. The three hundred smiling faces blur as she walks down the aisle into her future. He stands waiting at the altar, the look of love arcing the closing distance between them. They promise until death do us part.

"My daddy goed away," the three-year-old stammers to his grandmother, his blue eyes brimming. "My daddy cried, and my mommy cried. I cried, too."

He pops the complimentary champagne in the honeymoon suite, while she slips into the white peignoir she's tried on a hundred times. Rice from her clothes bounces off the tile bathroom floor, and she laughs out loud. We'll make our entire lives together one long honeymoon, she vows.

It's the walk, that certain, familiar swagger, that catches her eye. She glances up to see him reaching for the cereal at the end of the grocery-store aisle. She knows it's Cheerios. He always loved Cheerios. He hands the giant-size box to a woman, who tucks it into their cart. The simple domesticity of the little scene sends her fleeing from the store, ready to vomit. She remembers their first shopping trips together, list in hand and arms around each other. When had she stopped buying Cheerios?

Her white-knuckled fingers dig into his ring as she bears down yet again, her face contorting with the effort. The head crowns, then come the shoulders, and finally the feet. It's a boy! He looks at his son, and his eyes fill. Oh, the father he will be! The father he always wanted...

"You coddle those kids—they get away with murder," growls the newest man of her dreams, the one who swore he'd love to play daddy to another man's kids. "I'm never alone with you. Maybe they should go live with him. . . ." Her heart pumps furiously, trying to repair the damage of being ripped in half.

June brides and grooms, beware. Getting married is fun; being married is hard work. Slipping a golden band onto a finger does not guarantee she will never look at another man; it does not turn him into a person who easily confides his deepest feelings.

Listen to inner doubts or concerns expressed by family or friends. Take your time. You have such a long, long time to be married.

Or such a long, long time to be divorced.

**KEEP IT SIMPLE: Think ahead.**

## MAYBE IT'S NOT TOO LATE

"When two people are under the influence of the most violent, most insane, most delusive, and most transient of passions, they are required to swear that they will remain in that excited, abnormal, and exhausting condition continuously until death do them part."
—George Bernard Shaw

Shaw wrote that in 1908, but I can't help but wonder if such unrealistic expectations aren't responsible for today's high divorce rate. Perhaps we confuse instant attraction with love. We expect that first rush of feeling to last, to banish our problems, to carry us through some fantasy future.

And when it doesn't, we call it quits. Picked the wrong person, we tell friends. He's/she's no longer the person I married, we comfort ourselves. And we get a divorce and find a new love and start the cycle anew—until the rough times roll around and we realize—again—that we've made a mistake.

Maybe we haven't made a mistake. Maybe we simply don't give love a chance to ripen. Do we toss out a rosebud because it's "changed" by blossoming?

David and Kris would be celebrating their eighth anniversary—if they hadn't divorced four years ago when their children were just tots. Several love affairs later, they're now having long-distance talks on the phone.

They're discussing how much in love they were. And how young they were. What they did right—and wrong. How no one else can love your kids as much as the other parent. And what they've learned about themselves apart, and about life in general as they near thirty.

They're wondering if maybe, just maybe. But Kris is wary of promises she's heard before. David wants to be sure he can be the husband and father he longs to be. And I want to tell them,

"Move slowly. But give love a chance. Your kids deserve it—and you do, too."

Love is such a short word, yet it takes so long to develop. And only by allowing it to develop, by nurturing it, can we expect love to endure. I don't think that love fails us so much as we fail love.

To truly know one another—rather than the image we cast the other in—takes time. It takes history to bond us—all the good times we love to recall and the bad times we managed to weather.

Love is taking time off work when your wife's mother dies; holding your husband and allowing the tears when his best friend passes on. It's rushing to the hospital when your partner is thrown from a horse; his holding your hand as you wait for biopsy results on the lump in your breast.

Love is planning surprise birthday parties. It's nagging your mate to take vitamins. It's showing faith when one of you is laid off or fired. It's shared tears of joy over a newborn and worry when a child is ill. It's disagreement over disciplining a toddler, despair at having to put a teen into drug treatment, relief as you sit together at graduation.

Love is wondering what the heck you ever saw in him—and the next day wondering how you could ever live without him. It's knowing one another so well that you often finish each other's sentences, can tell immediately when something's wrong, can lip-sync the other's lines during the argument you've had a thousand times.

Love is the snoring that drives you nuts. It's hearing the same story yet again. It's wondering how your life would be different if you'd married someone else. It's sex that is sometimes routine. And it's also a warm bed on a cold morning, an unexpected well-spring of love when her key turns in the lock, and sometimes feeling so connected that lovemaking seems almost redundant.

Lasting love is arguing about where you'll go on vacation—and having someone to share the memories. It's lying awake wondering aloud together if you've done the right thing plunking down earnest money on your first house. It's questioning whether you'll make good parents as you both feel your unborn child kicking to get out. And, if you're lucky, it's grown kids regarding you as friends, little people shouting "Gramma" and "Grampa," cutting a silver or golden anniversary cake.

And—finally—love is feeling oh-so-lost on that endless drive home from the cemetery.

**KEEP IT SIMPLE: Realize that love deserves a second chance. Before it's too late.**

## A DOSE OF REALITY

Divorce is not a brief crisis, says Judith Wallerstein.

She and co-author Sandra Blakeslee blast that myth in the compelling book *Second Chances: Men, Women, and Children a Decade after Divorce.*

Believing that marriage is as easily discarded as wedding-gift wrapping is comforting, Wallerstein says.

"And it's comforting to think children react the same way," she adds.

She is the founder of the Center for Families in Transition, based in Corte Madera, California. She has studied sixty families who divorced in the '70s and '80s, interviewing members one year after their divorce and every five years thereafter.

The issue is not that we shouldn't ever divorce but that "we have to do divorce better on behalf of our children. Or we're failing divorce as well as marriage," Wallerstein says. "We have to realize the child needs more emotional and financial protection, access to both parents, and especially [the support of] two people who can treat each other with kindness."

Here are some of her findings:

- Young fathers visited their children less often than older dads. Children felt they had to be good or Dad wouldn't visit. Only 20 percent of the children had financial help with college from their fathers.

- Children of divorce felt robbed of their childhoods. They felt they had to take more responsibility; they were proud that they could but felt resentful they had to.

- The person who wanted out usually benefited most, getting a head start with either financial or emotional preparation in the final stage of the marriage.

- Men got back on track with their lives in about two and one-half years, but women took a year longer—perhaps because all the men who sought divorce had women waiting.

- Jumping into marriage again doesn't mean patterns change. One-half of the remarried men divorced again—their second wives wanted out—compared to a quarter of the women.

- When the mother remarried, boys usually rejoiced at gaining a stepfather, especially if he carefully cultivated relationships with the children. Girls were often reluctant, especially if they were very close to their mothers. Remarriage didn't affect the children as much as how the relationship changed with the custodial parent. Children did better if they felt included in the new union.

- Dad's remarriage affected kids less; they were often relieved someone would take care of him. Children, especially teens, were resentful for years if Dad married his mistress, even though this was never mentioned. Stepmothers who didn't make the children feel welcome were also resented.

So should we stay married, no matter what? No, says Wallerstein. But here's what we should do:

- Treat the dying marriage with respect. Don't be impulsive; make sure you've tried to make it work. Seek counseling first.

- Use counseling and mediation to resolve divorce disputes.

- Give yourself time to mourn the marriage. Seek help if you find yourself stuck in grief or anger.

- Recognize that divorce affects your children's lives forever. Give them explanations, help, and permission to love both parents.

- Stop fighting with your ex in front of the children; stop bad-mouthing him or her to the kids. Set a good example.

**KEEP IT SIMPLE:** Consider all options before divorcing.

## LETTING GO

Embarrassing as it is to admit, it's happened to most of us: We fall in love overnight. We become convinced we're soul mates. We wonder why it took this long to find each other. We radiate energy and goodwill. We even feel taller. Blithely, we tell the world: "I'm in love!"

We float through those first few weeks and months on a cloud. We talk on the phone for hours. Count the moments until we're together. Reinvent sex. Spend long moments just gazing into each other's eyes. Everything the other says is wonderfully witty and warm and wise. Past loves pale in comparison. "This is how life should be—and isn't," a friend said recently of new love. No wonder it's so glorious.

Oh, how we resent friends or family who suggest that maybe we're moving too quickly. Who hint that perhaps this person isn't as good for us as we think. Who remind us that we always fall in love too fast.

But, we huff, this is different! We're certainly old enough to know what we're doing. This isn't like anything that's ever happened before . . .

And then he doesn't call one evening. She leaves town without saying where she's going. He says he's not ready for a relationship. She says, "Let's just be friends," or the ever-popular, "It's not you, it's me." Or whatever.

A three-month wonder, one therapist calls these romances.

We are hurt and sad, frustrated and confused—and even angry. Some of us make pleading calls that later embarrass us. Others show up on doorsteps demanding explanations. We demand the return of every gift we ever gave, or we drive across town to return the *E* tile that dropped out of their Scrabble set. We write letters in the middle of the night.

Mark, forty-five, didn't mail his letter. It read:

"It is 1 A.M. Thursday. I am writing you this letter as I can't sleep and haven't been able to since Wednesday of last week when you informed me that you didn't think we should continue because I don't consider myself a Christian. I'm not sure that was the whole truth, but it must be one that you believe in because I think you are and have been as honest as you can be.

"I believe that what we experienced was addictive, codependent, and overwhelming and that for three months our lives got put on hold so that we could feel as if we had been rocketed into a fourth dimension. The love, compassion, understanding, and total acceptance we experienced . . . we both knew it was God's gift to us . . . .

"The times and special events—fly fishing, bike riding, rafting, watching the Perseid meteor shower, the jazz festival . . . and I don't and can't forget our lovemaking—are with me as if they all happened yesterday.

"The future looks pretty gray right now, but I'm confident there is a reason for all of this and we will look back someday as friends and smile at our memories. My belief is that when one door closes, and it has to close, God gives us a lesson and another door to open. I pray that we both learn our lessons before we open another door.

"I love you, and I'll miss you."

Like all of us who thought we had something special, only to lose it, Mark is hurt and must grieve. But he's also wise. He's keeping the split simple. He's not cajoling or threatening her into staying in the relationship. He's not vindictive or ugly. He's not blaming her for what went wrong. He's not bad-mouthing her.

He is letting her go in love, as agonizing as that is, knowing that with every love—however brief—there comes a treasure and something to be learned.

**KEEP IT SIMPLE: Remember that hearts do heal.**

## TAKING CARE OF YOURSELF

Like taxes, the lows of love are here to stay. But when your heartbeat's a deadbeat, there are some things you can do to stay emotionally afloat.

*Simplify your life.* Now's the time to stick to the basics, to weed out the activities, people, and responsibilities that overwhelm you during this vulnerable period. Unless you welcome the diversion, say no to activities that will tax you, physically or emotionally. Establish a simple routine to give shape to your day; routine can bring security. Look for simple pleasures that will help get you back in touch with the world: walking, swimming, watching children at play, lingering over the newspaper. Enjoy a simple treat each day, such as a latte, a new magazine, or a chat with a friend.

*Focus on yourself, not him or her.* Stop reading his horoscope. Don't listen to the songs she loves. Phone a friend instead of dialing your lover's number just to hear that voice on the answering machine. Instead of asking yourself what he or she is doing now, ask yourself: If I weren't sitting here being miserable, what would I be doing? What did I enjoy before I got involved with this person? Get a life, independent of your lover.

*Avoid nostalgia.* When we operate from nostalgia, we usually remember only the good aspects of the relationship. To keep things in balance, list the reasons the relationship wasn't healthy or satisfying for you. Tack a copy of that list near the phone (or carry it in your wallet), and read it when you're tempted to make that futile phone call.

*Make a "busy list."* When you're feeling OK, list things that need doing. Then when you freak out and want to call or drive over to see your ex (to fight, make up, etc.), consult the list and get busy.

The list might include these tasks: clean out jewelry box, reorganize garage (or linen cupboard or kitchen cupboard), alphabetize spices or records, organize the bookcase by topic. Each task will keep you constructively occupied, make life a tad easier, and—most importantly—prevent reverting to behavior you'll probably regret.

This list proved a lifesaver for me during a difficult separation from my husband. We don't want to stay so busy that we don't feel our emotions, but we do want to divert ourselves from acting foolishly.

*Nurture yourself.* We can torture ourselves—which is a certain way to give someone else a lot of power over us—or we can be good to ourselves. What would make you feel good right now (besides that)? Neglecting ourselves is giving away personal power. Hungry to be touched? Get a massage. Lonely? Call a friend or invite a pal to a movie. Having a tough time with the week? Prepare for Friday night or Sunday afternoon by making plans with supportive people. Hate to eat alone? Buy your favorite foods, set the table beautifully for one (use a placemat and a napkin ring and a wine goblet), light a candle, and put on your favorite music. (If you have kids, they'll enjoy this, too.) Remove that obviously empty chair. Eat slowly and tell yourself you deserve the best.

*Seek out a higher power.* It's tempting to make a man or woman we love into God, giving him or her total power over our lives. We keep things in perspective when we realize there's something bigger than us or another person. Strive to see the bigger picture and your place in it. Even though we don't see it during a crisis, great good may come from this. We may finally be free of a relationship that wasn't good for us. We'll learn more about ourselves, and we'll be free to meet someone more suited to us.

*Keep a journal.* Pour out your feelings on paper, in private. This is helpful to reread when your willpower weakens or you're overcome with nostalgia. Journaling jumbled emotions through separation and reconciliation helped me immeasurably. Writing it gave me a place to vent my pain and frustration and enabled me to see the patterns in our relationship (both healthy and destructive). My journal provided encouragement as my situation began to improve. I found that reading aloud portions of my journal to my partner helped me communicate more clearly.

*Try helping others.* An old saying states that the best way to beat the blues is to do something for someone else. It really works. We also increase our self-worth, realizing that we're important to others.

*Surrender.* Remember, we have no control over others. Your lover may or may not see the light, come back, or mend his or her ways. When we're able to accept the outcome without trying to force it, we achieve serenity. Now's the time to be philosophical: If it's meant to be, it will be.

*Acknowledge your feelings.* Of course, we're going to feel anxious, angry, and sad. That's part of being human. But we get into trouble when we act on those feelings inappropriately (going to our lover's workplace and making a scene, which makes us look like an idiot) or try to repress them (and getting depressed or sick instead). Better to face it and feel it. We can cry when we feel sad, or write an angry letter—and not mail it.

*Seek supportive people.* During tough times, we're tempted to hole up with our hurt. Embarrassment at having a lover leave can drive us deeper into our cave of isolation. Now's the time when we need to reach out for support and reassurance that we're still lovable and worthwhile. To support us, we need friends who will listen and acknowledge our feelings; they don't have to agree that our lover's a jerk. Don't succumb to what I call the Everybody's-at-the-Orgy-But-Me Syndrome. It may be 7 P.M. Saturday, but not everyone is out on a romantic fling. Keep calling till you find somebody home who wants to do something fun.

*Be confident you will survive.* One of the good things about getting older is learning that we do not die if things—including love—don't go the way we want. We can survive and even learn from the experience.

*Make a relationship list.* In your journal or elsewhere, make a list of what you need in a relationship. It might read: "A sense of humor. Being able to say whatever's on my mind. A shared love of travel. A sense my world is broadening and not narrowing. Freedom to have friends without jealousy." The list you come up with will help you get clear on what is most important as you become open to new relationships. And it can also pinpoint what your previous relationship lacked.

*Know that you will love again.* Again, look to the past. How many times before did you despair when romance turned sour? And it either worked out and you strengthened the relationship, or you eventually moved on to love someone new.

Here's a simple exercise some therapists recommend to avoid bitterness and keep life in perspective. Before drifting off to sleep (or anytime you start to hurt), whisper, "I love you, I bless you, I let you go." Say it regularly until you mean it. My husband did it daily, augmented with a slightly bitter "May Jann get what she truly deserves." Now we laugh that what Jann truly deserves is him!

A ruptured romance isn't fun, but it can propel us on our journey of discovery. It will get better.

**KEEP IT SIMPLE: Live and learn.**

## GETTING "CUSTODY" OF DIVORCING FRIENDS

You've suspected something was up. Her smile seemed forced through a sieve. His brusque "everything's fine" manner fit like a cheap suit. And then you find out why: Your friends are splitting up.

While it's their divorce, you feel the pain. Maybe you've been through it yourself, but—darn it—somebody's dream of happy-ever-after is supposed to come true.

So how do you deal with your disillusionment and remain a supportive friend?

When people we care about are hurting, our own unresolved pain is easily tapped. If you find yourself overreacting to your friend's pain (bursting into tears at odd times, thinking about their situation constantly, getting angry with them or their spouse), you probably have unfinished business with your own divorce (or perhaps your parents'). Consider talking to a therapist about it.

Just as a friend's death reminds us of our own mortality, a separation or divorce can lay bare some fears or insecurities about our own relationships. Divorce is no more contagious than cancer, but people often act as if it were. Use your friend's situation to become even closer to your spouse by discussing your fears.

These guidelines may help:

*Don't choose sides.* It's tempting but troubling to do so—and unfair when you hear only one side of the story. Tell each that you care about them both.

*Don't bad-mouth the other's spouse.* They might do this to you, but don't add your character assessment to the crossfire. Saying "I've always thought he was a jerk and wondered why you stuck with him" will be tough words to live with if the couple reunites.

*Don't give advice.* Only the people involved can decide the best action for them.

*Don't drop your friends.* Arrange to see them separately. Separation or divorce is a big-enough change in a person's life without losing the company of valued friends as well.

*Don't let your friends' divorce come between you and your spouse.* It's easy for the woman to identify with the wife's viewpoint and for the man to relate to the husband's—but don't let it create a rift between you. Neither of you is responsible for the other man's or woman's actions or feelings; you don't have to attack or defend. One feuding couple is enough.

*Listen.* Be sympathetic but don't offer advice unless specifically asked.

*Let them know you care.* Sometimes people can't share their pain, and they isolate themselves from friends. Make contact periodically to say: "I care about you." "I'm praying that everything works out for the best." "I'm here if you want to talk—it's OK to call, even in the middle of the night."

*Share your own relevant experience.* Saying what helped you is not the same as advice-giving. Discuss your regrets about having an affair, your experience with a particular divorce attorney, your problems with the kids, your discovery that your bitterness dissipated with time.

*Encourage each person to take care of himself or herself.* Offer to exercise with them, urge them to have a pampering massage—but don't join them in drinking binges.

*Maintain neutrality.* Don't carry tales or messages between the two warring spouses. On the other hand, don't get embroiled in the feud by agreeing to keep secrets.

*Set limits to take care of yourself.* If one person's bad-mouthing of their spouse becomes too much for you, say, "I understand you're really upset. But I think you need to find someone else to vent your anger on. It's really hard for me to hear it." If one person wants you to meet their new love and you're uncomfortable with this, say, "I care about you—but I'm just not ready for that yet. Maybe later."

*Realize that you may lose a friend.* Some people demand such fierce loyalty that they can't tolerate your continued association with their former spouse. Playing fair could cost you.

If the divorcing parties are very close to you—best friends or parents—it may be necessary to tell them that you just can't listen because you feel too closely involved. Suggest they see a counselor instead.

**KEEP IT SIMPLE: Show sympathy and don't judge.**

## COPING WITH YOUR PARENTS' DIVORCE

When our parents divorce, it creates a dichotomy.

As adults we may understand—especially if we've been through a divorce of our own. But the child inside may feel hurt, confused, or even abandoned as we give up the fairy tale of a perfect family.

My parents' divorce when I was thirty-five caused more pain than my own divorce had. As an adult I could see the dynamics of what went wrong. But it hurt like crazy.

In our pain, it helps to remember two things: One, the divorce is about our parents, not about us—even though we're affected. We are not flawed; it is not a rejection of us. And two, we are not alone in our confusion and pain. Just talk to those who've been through it; look at the new books on the subject.

Here are some rough times we may go through:

*Each parent talks about the other.* I tried to listen, advise, and be sympathetic—but it was too much for the little kid inside. I finally told both that they needed to confide in someone else.

*We're invited to meet our parent's new partner.* If you're not ready for this big step, say so. Seeing our parent with someone new after a longtime marriage isn't easy. A sister was with me when we first met my father's intended wife. We were able to support each other and to discuss favorable changes we saw in our dad.

*Our siblings take sides.* Divorce affects each grown child differently. Those who live the closest are most likely to get caught in the crossfire and might choose sides. Parents may try to manipulate us into this. When brothers and sisters talk openly with each other about their feelings, the war might be confined to mom and dad.

*We're invited to the wedding.* Having a parent remarry is usually concrete proof that our parents will never get back together. Dad begged me to come to his wedding, while Mom insisted it would be a slap in her face if I went. Attending the ceremony was one of the toughest things I ever did—supported, again, by one of my sisters. It hurt all the way through—I kept seeing my mother in the place of the bride—though we got support from two couples who were longtime family friends.

But all experiences can be used for good. When I became a second wife a few years later, I knew exactly how my new husband's grown children felt and fully appreciated the special gift they gave their father by their presence.

*We attend the first family occasion after the split or remarriage.* The first time I visited my mother after my parents' divorce, it felt like a funeral. There was their furniture, but my dad wasn't walking into the room. I burst into tears at the realization. Later, I came to enjoy watching my mother bloom as she redecorated and made her own life.

When one parent remarries, he or she may want to pretend that it's the same old happy family gathering. (Those of us who have remarried may have done this, too.) But we grown children are aware of that new daddy doll slipped into our dad's place. We can expect some awkwardness. The gatherings often become more comfortable over time—and might even be fun!

*We acquire stepbrothers or stepsisters.* When my father remarried, he had a teenage stepdaughter the age of my own daughters. The first time I called, they were lying on the floor playing Monopoly. That stung. I couldn't remember him playing it with me. At the same time, the adult me could appreciate how nice it was for this girl to have a father to play games with.

Ultimately we need to remember that just as we want our parents to accept the person we choose, so we need to accept their choices. It's not about renouncing one parent; it's about accepting reality.

And reality changes. My father divorced his second wife, Mom died, and he remarried—on the other side of the world. It gets easier.

**KEEP IT SIMPLE:** Honoring decisions works both ways between parent and child.

## When Your Adult Child Separates

Perhaps it came as a surprise, or maybe you saw it brewing. Neither is easy. Your child is hurting, and so are you.

If your own marriage has endured, you wonder why "the kids" can't work out their problems as you did yours. If divorce is against your religion, you may worry about your child's standing in the church—or in your friends' estimation.

If you've been divorced, you understand intellectually the failure of a marriage, but emotionally there's pain. You wanted the fairy tale to come true for someone—especially a child you hold dear.

In either case, you may wonder: Where did I fail? Did I set a lousy example, turn a deaf ear when my child needed to talk, contribute to the divorce by helping too much or too little?

If you have grandchildren, the pain is magnified: How will they be affected? Will I lose contact with them?

Here are some general things to keep in mind:

*Understand that you can't make another person—not even your grown child—do anything.* Mental-health professionals point out that your son or daughter must do what he or she feels is right. Acceptance is always simpler than fighting in vain and blaming others for years afterward.

*Expect to grieve.* You may be sad, angry, or ashamed as your child's divorce brings up your own feelings of failure. Give yourself time to heal; talk about it with a friend.

*Let your child know you care.* You can show support by voicing confidence in his or her ability to "do the right thing." Help is only destructive if you "enable"—doing for them what they should be doing for themselves.

*Don't take sides.* Blood may be thicker than water, but try to offer your child support without actually taking sides. If you blame one, you'll be embarrassed—and perhaps resented—if the couple reconciles.

*Continue your relationships.* You may still visit with a beloved in-law who's become an "ex-law"—perhaps privately if your child is resentful. Don't be surprised if that relationship fades when your child remarries; handling an "in" and an "ex" may prove difficult. But it is possible—I'm doing it. It's good for my grandchildren to be on good terms with their father and his folks. Because I live near the kids, and the other set of grandparents is in another state, I pass on stories about the children and the artwork they've done.

*Set limits and rules if your divorced child moves home.* Make a time limit, rent agreement, chore list, and house rules you can all live with. If you lend money, be up front about whether it's a gift or a loan and under what terms you expect to be paid.

*Support your grandchildren.* They need you now. Serve as a sounding board for them, but don't criticize either parent. Help out, but remember that your child has primary responsibility for and authority over them. Consider asking your child to incorporate your visitation rights into the divorce decree. Many states protect grandparents' rights. Check out what yours are.

**KEEP IT SIMPLE: Be supportive and bite your tongue.**

## DIVORCE IS NEVER REALLY OVER

So you're considering divorce?

It's easy.

After all, he won't share his feelings, and she's impossible, and nothing should have to be this much work. The kids cry when you tell them you're splitting, but they'll get over it.

So one moves out, and the living room has some gaps in it, but it's not so bad until you get the Christmas boxes down to divide the decorations, and you go through the albums and pull some photos so your ex can have a set. And the sheriff's deputy serves papers written in cold legalese.

You go home every night to an empty house, or to a bar or a department store so you don't have to face the emptiness. Or you dash off to day care to pick up the kids, and there's no one to help you when they're driving you crazy, and you drop into bed so tired that you feel you'll never wake up.

Suddenly you're not invited to the big Christmas get-together, and you never see your father-in-law, who'd seemed so much like the dad you never had, and you miss all those folks, but after all, blood is thicker than water. Maybe you didn't divorce just one person...

You go to school programs and beam with pride at your child on stage, but there's no one to nudge and share it with, and suddenly you feel so alone. The kids come to visit every other weekend, and you knock yourself out trying to entertain them, wondering why it feels so forced. And you wonder: What on earth did we do on weekends when we all lived together?

Then your ex remarries and comes to pick up the kids for the wedding. Everyone is cruising through life but you. You wonder if your kids will love the new stepparent more than you, and you know that's crazy, but still...

You find yourself snapping at the kids and being petty when they come home talking about your ex and the new spouse, the new gifts they got, how they never fight, and how they are always holding hands and being lovey.

Your ex moves out of state, and you see the kids even less. Plus you have to ante up to fly them out summers and every other Christmas. These dear little strangers troop off the plane, and as thrilled as you are to see them, you hold back a piece of your heart so it won't hurt so badly when they leave. It doesn't really help, because each time they go home, it's like ripping a scab off a wound that never seems to heal.

You date, but it's hard to find much privacy. It's easier not to have much of a social life, to focus on the kids instead. And before you know it, they don't want to be seen at the movies with you on a Saturday night and even suggest that you get a life of your own.

But hope springs eternal, and you finally remarry, only to discover that the people involved aren't a plastic dollhouse family ready to automatically fit your expectations. Here are the same old marital problems, complicated by two sets of kids. If my kids are away this weekend and yours are here, when do we have time alone?

Then a child graduates, and you have a family dinner out, each end of the table anchored by a parent and stepparent, and the kids aren't sure where to sit. It's an awkward rehearsal for a child's wedding later on.

Just for a moment as the bride and her father walk down the aisle, your eyes lock with his, and you know you're both thinking of that day you brought her home, petrified because neither of you knew how to change diapers. And in that moment, all the years you didn't share in these precious children's lives hit you in the stomach, but you keep smiling.

And afterward, even though your ex's mate grumbles about it, you and your ex pose with your children, all grown up and dressed up—a family portrait twenty-some years overdue. The kids thank you for making it happen. At last, a picture with both their parents.

Later, at another family occasion, your eyes fill as you watch your grandchildren clamber over your ex—the grandparent they so seldom see. You remember Sunday-night dinners at your own grandparents' home, the couple who went together like salt-and-pepper shakers. You wonder who was cheated more, you or your kids or your grandchildren.

You make a pretense of snapping crowd shots, but then you stop worrying about what his wife will think, and you zero in for a close-up of your grandson sitting on his grandpa's lap. The years telescope, and you are young parents with your babies again—back when your hopes were high, and the promise of forever didn't ring false.

**KEEP IT SIMPLE:** Know that a divorce may be easy to get, but it's never final.

# 6. FALLIN' IN LOVE AGAIN: REMARRIAGE

*Those who have loved once or twice already are so much the better educated.*
—Robert Louis Stevenson

So you're ready to middle-aisle it again.

Congratulations.

You're older now, and your head and heart have grown wiser. You've learned from the past. And you deserve happiness! But you also have your work cut out. Subsequent marriages have a high failure rate.

When we remarry, one or both of us often bring children. We drag along old emotional baggage. We might have other prior responsibilities, at least financially if not emotionally. And not all of us have realized that it takes two to make or break a marriage; we might not have changed the patterns which contributed to a previous marital split.

Yet faith thrives in the human heart. With love, work, a sense of humor, and a healthy dose of realism, we can find the happiness that escaped us the first time around.

## IN THIS CIRCLE OF LOVE

*Love.*

We form our notions of love early, depending on what we see at home, on television, and in the movies.

In junior high, we experience it for the first time. Like wow, I feel like my stomach is in my throat whenever I see him, and we both love pepperoni pizza and bowling!

Then there's high school, with an even greater number of hormones zinging through our smooth young bodies. This must be love because we talk on the phone endlessly and park in the dark for hours. And his parents don't understand him any more than mine do me, ya know? The more cerebral might help each other with homework, or at least use that as an excuse to be together.

Our hearts are broken for the first time, and maybe we learn that unrequited love isn't just something in an eleventh-grade English-class poem by old what's-his-name.

Come college, we're free of parental restrictions. Idealism competing with glands, we find a love who shares our political cause, our spiritual quest, or our hell-bent rebellion against the establishment. We talk long into the night, solving the problems of the universe. The sheer headiness of that competes with sex.

And before long, we marry, confident we know what love is. After all, we're grown-ups now. And marriage is what grown-ups do.

We float down the aisle in a cloud of organza, hopes high because we've read those women's magazines, and we know how to keep him interested forever, balance career and motherhood, lose weight, and make these luscious thirty-minute recipes.

The honeymoon pictures are pasted in the album, and the work begins. For many of us, disillusionment sets in. He's different. He's not attentive. Or reading my mind. Or meeting my needs. Or doing his share of the housework. We hardly talk anymore, except about the kids. (Of course, he has his own list about us.)

And the articles in the women's magazines don't help. If only he'd change, we tell friends. But he doesn't, and we move on, taking the kids and continuing to hiss our grievances over the phone.

We swear off love and content ourselves with work, kids, and the occasional dinner out with a girlfriend. You can't trust men, right? And yet, sometimes it's so lonely.

We give love another chance. Hey, his first wife sounds as bad as my first husband. This time, marriage will work. Sure, the kids will all get along great. We've learned from our mistakes, haven't we?

But the kids don't all get along great. And can't we have just one meal together without your ex calling to whine about something? We're torn between our children and our second chance.

We see a counselor and wail away at the relationship. You need to get a grip on your kid and stop fixating on mine. Well, yes, I did have this particular problem in my first marriage, but it's not part of a pattern or anything I need to look at. OK, we'll practice saying, "When you..., I feel...."

Not wanting to fail again, we continue to try to fit square pegs into round holes. Still blaming the other, we sign on the dotted line for Split Number Two.

If we're smart, we're not bitter. Instead of trashing our ex, we take a good long look at ourselves, get some professional help, and identify the patterns of finding someone to rescue or someone who will rescue us, of focusing on another's needs to the exclusion of our own, of believing that it's someone else's job to make us happy, of thinking that someone else should change, could change, if only we love them enough or vice versa.

We realize that the only person we can control is ourselves. We struggle to change, to gain a clearer sense of who we are, what we want, what we consider important.

And one day, when we least expect it—and weren't even looking—there stands someone who has been doing the very same thing.

Having nothing to lose (certainly never again our sense of self), we say exactly what we think. Expose precisely who we are. Talk and listen in equal amounts. Feel heard and perceived.

We are energized, not drained. Our world broadens instead of narrows. We find ourselves risking and trusting. Instead of trying to manipulate and control, we simply let go.

We look into the soul of another and see our own shining back at us—our light reflected, not refracted.

*Love.*

**KEEP IT SIMPLE: Know you have a second chance.**

## CREATING A SECOND FAMILY

You're single, you've got kids, and you're dating—maybe even looking for a mate. Or maybe you don't have kids, and you're leery of dating someone who does.

Subsequent marriages have a high failure rate, and children are a big factor in whether a remarriage swims or sinks.

Be sensible: Consider the problems and rewards of step-parenting before becoming one of the 1,800 stepfamilies forming daily.

### DATING AS A PARENT

If you or the person you're dating have children, here are some considerations:

*Should I tell him/her right away that I have kids?* This is a touchy subject for many single parents. Some figure it's better to wait until the other person is truly interested in you before breaking the big news. Others reason that there's no point in being deceptive; telling the truth weeds out the noncontenders quickly.

Kerry, a twenty-seven-year-old single mother, advises: "By the end of the evening of the first date, you should tell them. If they don't call you again, that means you don't want them anyway, because they have no interest in your children—and the kids come first."

*Who makes the best stepparent: someone with or without his or her own kids?* Again, it depends. A parent will, one hopes, have an understanding of children and the work they require. On the other hand, he or she has emotional baggage—and often a lot of guilt, if child visits are only periodic. He or she might feel resentment at spending more time with your kids than with their own.

A person without kids is free to lavish time and attention on your kids. But will they want to? Are they prepared to make the concessions necessary? Are they willing to share your time and attention?

Herb had never married. But when he did at forty-four, it was to a woman with grown children. He'd been wary of women with young children before: "They have lots of needs, and I didn't want to subordinate mine to theirs."

Nine years later, Herb speaks of "our daughters" and "our grandchildren." He's glad he did it, despite his reservations: "I feel loved and admired, but a part of me always wishes I could have done more, that I could have been freer and more easygoing with lots of money to spend. But that isn't what my family considers most important."

Herb's advice: "Try it. A lot of deserving people—both the parents and the children—are dying on the vine a little each day because someone can't or won't reach out and try to share a life with them. I don't mean it in the charity sense, but don't rule out someone with children. They have the power to enrich your life and open up areas you didn't even imagine existed."

*Beware of someone too eager to embrace your children.* Whether man or woman, this could be a severely codependent person who wants to "rescue" you and your kids. George admits he married a woman with several kids because he thought he could help her— not a good reason to marry, he said after the divorce.

I once dated a schoolteacher who barreled into my home ready to "play school" with my kids. Rob didn't understand that you don't snap off the television in the middle of a favorite program to have a story hour.

One young single parent cautions about dates who are "overly nice, buying the kids presents all the time. They might be trying to win you over. A lot of people will do anything to get to you— including going through your kids."

A person looking for a ready-made family might have unrealistic expectations about raising children. Or (worst case), he could be a pedophile looking for young children to seduce. (Beware of the adult who spends more time with the kids than with you.)

*On the other hand, be cautious of the person who seems to merely tolerate your kids for your sake.* Michelle, a mother of three who lived with such a man, caught her mistake before marrying him.

She realized that trying to get him to take responsibility for and be interested in her kids was more trouble than parenting alone. And she saw that it hurt her kids to be continually rebuffed when they asked him to play catch or read a story.

Michelle advises: "Beware of the people who always want the kids out of the way—shoving them into another room or telling them to go outside. If he or she is too busy for them, watch out. You have to have someone interested in family life—'cause that's what it is with kids. It's a package deal."

## Children of blended families

As adults, we go into remarriage feeling older and wiser. But that doesn't mean our children are.

They might still be mourning the divorce or a dead parent—or resenting us for leaving. Or perhaps we've finally succeeded in healing their confusion and anger only to have them feel abandoned all over again as we clasp a new love—and perhaps other children—to our hearts.

How children receive the big news depends on their age, the circumstances of the divorce, the length of the separation, and our closeness to them. Tiny tots might be thrilled to have a daddy in the house again; teens used to their autonomy might resent a new authority figure on the scene. A child who's felt responsible for either parent's welfare might feel relieved at sharing the responsibility—or jealous at being displaced.

In our own excitement about a second chance at happily-ever-after, we may also forget that we each bring old baggage into this new union. We have not only the image of marriage we received from our parents but also the one we developed with our first mates.

And we're likely to continue playing out our old roles unless we consciously break them through working on ourselves or seeking couples' counseling. (Many modern couples do this before marrying.)

Here are some suggestions for simplifying the formation of stepfamilies:

- Move to a different home—one that is new to you both. Give the kids some choices, such as what colors their rooms will be painted.

- Include the children in the wedding so they feel part of this new union. Family medallions to present to children—as well as a written ceremony that includes them—are available from Clergy Services (see Resources).

- Have the child's own parent handle discipline for the first few months. Trying to shape up your mate's kids will only foster resentment and make you the bad guy.

- Realize that children will be torn in their loyalties between the stepparent and the original parent. Help the child know that to love one parent doesn't mean the child must stop loving the other. Parents can help by not bad-mouthing the other parent to the child.

- Foster equality among his kids and her kids by periodically rotating chores and bedrooms so that no one is stuck with the dirtiest job or the smallest room.

- Learn about each family's history by sharing photo albums and old home movies.

- Try to incorporate the customs of both families for holidays and birthdays. Gradually, you'll create new traditions.

- Consider holding weekly or monthly family meetings where it is safe for everyone to express feelings and discuss problems without reprisal.

- Don't let the children divide you as a couple. They may try, through manipulation and guilt. And make time for yourselves alone.

- Get to know a stepchild better or maintain closeness with your child through periodic times alone in an activity you both enjoy.

- Be kind but firm. Your ex-spouse may feel threatened by your remarriage. Focus on what's best for the children.

- Create a firm bond among the stepsiblings. Eventually having a new child may give them something in common. But having a child too soon might create problems; make sure your marriage is stable first.

- Avoid treating the kids as a crowd. They are each individuals with their own special needs, talents, and feelings.

KEEP IT SIMPLE: Realize that a family isn't formed overnight.

Ah, summer. The season of lemonade, swims, and stepkids.

What the natural parent anticipates all year can be a time of stress for the stepparent. Suddenly your routine is scrambled by the invasion of small people who may look a lot like the person you love.

You may even love them too, but...

Sometimes you find yourself jealous of your spouse's attention to them. Resentful of the comparisons they make between you and the mom or dad they left at home. And irritated that your solitude is shot or that your limited time with your own children and mate must be shared.

Well, summer visits to their "other home" isn't a picnic for the kids, either.

The Stepfamily Association of America (see Resources) cites these stressors for children:

- Hearing the original parents argue and being used as a pawn or messenger between them.

- Resenting orders from the stepparent.

- Feeling blamed for everything that goes wrong.

- Not being able or allowed to see the natural parent, and resenting the stepparent for it.

- Hearing the parent and stepparent fight and worrying that this marriage will break up, too.

- Seeing their parents do more for the stepchildren than for them.

- Having stepsiblings intruding on their space or privacy.

- Feeling unwanted—which is often a test to see if either family wants them.

- Feeling angry and depressed and wishing things were back the way they were before divorce or death.

- Feeling responsibility for making the new family work.

- Adjusting to new household rules.

So what are some things all parents—mother, father, and stepmom or stepdad—can do to make the visit more satisfying? (Let's assume that the kids are leaving their mother to visit their father, as most—but not all—children do.)

The parent sending the children to visit can

- Send the kids off with a positive attitude about the good time they'll have—and properly equipped (sufficient clean clothes, toys to keep them occupied en route, stamped postcards to send home or to friends, etc.).

- Assure the kids that you won't feel threatened if they love Dad's new wife or have a good time.

- Acknowledge that the rules at the other home might be different but must be followed.

The parent receiving the children for the visit can

- Clarify with your partner what things you'll be doing for your kids and what things you'd like help with and when. Give your partner a voice in the matter—and express your gratitude for the help you get.

- Discipline the kids when they need it—and do it yourself so the stepparent doesn't become the heavy.

- Realize that children need your time and attention more than they need new toys and constant entertainment. They need you, not more stuff. Do what you'd normally do if the kids lived with you.

- Reserve time alone together without the children so your relationship isn't compromised.

And the stepparent can

- Extend yourself lovingly and willingly, knowing that this won't last forever—and that your partner will feel less torn if you cooperate.

- Give your partner time alone with the kids and use the free time to do something for yourself.

- Don't bad-mouth the other parent or nose into how things were before the divorce—but do be a good listener if the child needs to talk.

- Try to be a grown-up friend to the children instead of a mother-substitute—unless they are looking for one.

All three parties should remember not to grill the kids about each other. And don't expect miracles or try for, or demand, perfection.

Then comes this question: How can we sustain the renewed closeness with our child?

A young father I know, Shawn Julian of Citrus Heights, California, takes plenty of pictures while his two children are visiting and then has double prints made. He buys an inexpensive album with magnetic pages and assembles a memory book of the kids from their time with him. The kids love it and can relive their visit—and his love—anytime they feel lonely.

Or, we could give our child an empty album and send a new picture every week and let them assemble it themselves. They might want to collect postcards, ticket stubs, menus, or match-book covers during the visit to add to the album.

Phone calls, weekly letters, funny greeting cards, postcards, and audiotapes or videotapes can help us keep in touch between visits. Dollar bills, baseball cards, or even sticks of gum tucked into an envelope are welcome surprises.

The most important thing is letting our kids know we care: out of sight does not mean out of mind.

Even when they're not here, they're at home in our hearts.

KEEP IT SIMPLE: Circumstances change, but parenthood is forever.

Some thirty family members—including three of their five grown children—stood smiling in the park's rose garden on July 2, 1988, to witness Dick and Patty Montgomery say "I do."

Again.

The couple had come a long way since they were first married in a Presbyterian church on June 10, 1955. Five children. Career changes. Her return to school. A divorce after twenty-five years. His four-year second marriage. And a lot of personal growth.

The Montgomerys are among the 1 percent of divorced people who remarry each other—just like Elizabeth Taylor and Richard Burton, and Natalie Wood and Robert Wagner.

Others, for whom no statistics are available, divorce and then date, "go steady," or even live together without formally retying the knot.

One in ten couples will separate and reconcile at least once during their marriage, statisticians say. A quarter return home within a week; another quarter take five or more months to come back.

Whatever the circumstances, therapists warn that unless couples work at changing their old patterns of relating, the union is likely to fail again. And a revolving-door marriage can renew the pain for parents and children.

"When you come back, you're risking doing that brutal thing to the children all over again if you decide to split," says David Worthington, a clinical psychologist in a marriage and family clinic. Marriage counselors say that breakups are most often caused by unskilled communication, one person's spurt of emotional growth, or a mid-life crisis—sometimes with the grass-is-greener syndrome.

The Montgomerys' reasons might fit all three. After a rough year in 1980, they postponed celebrating their twenty-fifth anniversary till the next year. Next year never came.

Dick was struggling to support his big family in the highly competitive advertising field, but basically he was happy.

Patty recalls a "typical '50s marriage in which I submerged myself as wife and mother and lost myself. I emerged about forty, really needing to grow and change, and there wasn't space in the marriage for that." At forty-eight, she left and went back to school in San Francisco for her doctorate in East-West psychology.

Dick, who had remarried and divorced, got a call one day from Patty. She was taking some personal-growth training and "had some cleaning up to do of old, angry feelings so we could be friends."

They met for several hours, and Patty realized that "there was a deeply loving connection that had gotten covered over with all the garbage. We really like each other a lot, and we were wise and mature enough to forgive each other and ourselves.

"We both took responsibility," she says today, "for what we did and didn't do in the marriage."

A year later, when she finished school, they remarried. In their sixties, they do things differently. They try to take responsibility for their behavior and their own happiness instead of blaming or expecting the other to provide happiness. They enjoy their careers, she as a college teacher and consultant on women's issues, he as a public-relations man.

She has learned the importance of being true to herself, following her spiritual guidance, and taking care of herself.

He has "come to grips with 'judgmentalism.' Once I got it through my head not to judge her, her life, or her values, but to work on myself—that was the breakthrough and speeded the healing. I've learned to have faith and stop analyzing."

Couples reunite for many reasons. Those who remarry, Worthington says, often feel a strong attraction that doesn't dissipate over the years. But such couples often are opposite personality types. He cites Taylor and Burton—strong attraction combined with poor communication, "so when they're apart, they gravitate together, but when they're together, they eventually explode."

Couples who live together but don't remarry, he finds, tend to be people who are drawn to each other but because of past experience are hesitant to fully commit.

Unless a couple changes how they communicate, therapists say, separation is likely.

"I find that when a couple who really cares about one another develops good communication skills, the rest takes care of itself," says Worthington. "Each circumstance varies, but the honeymoon will end, the way it did last time. And what you have left is two people needing to understand each other and appreciate their differences rather than berate one another for them."

For people considering reconciliation, the experts advise counseling first. Don't make rash decisions. Move slowly.

And those who've been there say: Give the marriage another chance so you can feel you really tried. State your wants and needs directly instead of expecting your partner to guess. Be honest with each other. Give each other time alone.

As Patty Montgomery puts it, "There's a rhythm to marriage—good and not-so-good—and you have to allow that."

The Montgomerys' journey had come full circle, as they noted in the T. S. Eliot quotation from their second wedding invitation:

We shall not cease from exploration
And the end of all our exploring
Will be to arrive where we started
And know the place for the first time.

KEEP IT SIMPLE: Honor your heart's history.

# BIBLIOGRAPHY

De Angelis, Barbara. *The Real Rules: How to Find the Right Man for the Real You*. New York: Dell, 1997.

Fisher, Helen. *Anatomy of Love: The Mysteries of Mating, Marriage, and Why We Stray*. New York: Norton, 1994.

Goldberg, Herb. *What Men Really Want*. New York: Penguin Books, 1991.

Houston, Victoria. *Loving a Younger Man: How Women Are Finding and Enjoying a Better Relationship*. Chicago: Contemporary Books, 1987.

James, Jennifer. *Women and the Blues: Passions That Hurt, Passions That Heal*. San Francisco: Harper & Row, 1988.

Jeffers, Susan. *The Journey from Lost to Found: The Search That Begins with the End of a Relationship*. New York: Ballantine, 1993.

———. *Opening Our Hearts to Men*. New York: Ballantine, 1989.

Reed-Jones, Carol. *Green Weddings That Don't Cost the Earth*. Bellingham, Wash.: Paper Crane Press, 1996.

Wallerstein, Judith, and Sandra Blakeslee. *Second Chances: Men, Women, and Children a Decade after Divorce.* New York: Houghton Mifflin, 1996.

# Resources

## Age discrepancies
Wives of Older Men
1029 Sycamore Ave.
Tinton Falls, NJ 07701
(908) 747-5586

*International networking support group for younger women married to older men. Annual membership of $35 includes bimonthly newsletter.*

## Child-free partnerships
Childless by Choice
P.O. Box 695
Leavenworth, WA 98826
(509) 763-2112
76206.3216@compuserve.com

*This group offers literature for childless and "still-deciding" people.*

ENVIRONMENTAL WEDDINGS
*Green Weddings Newsletter*
P.O. Box 29292
Bellingham, WA 98228-1292

*The quarterly newsletter is $4 annually.*

INTERFAITH MARRIAGES
*Crosswinds: The Newsletter about Interfaith Relationships*
American River, Inc.
P.O. Box 429422
Cincinnati, OH 45242-9422

*A one-year subscription (six issues) is $15.95.*

*Dovetail: A Newsletter by and for Jewish-Christian Families*
Dovetail Publishing
P.O. Box 19945
Kalamazoo, MI 49019

*A one-year subscription (six issues) is $24.99.*

ROMANCE

*The RoMANtic*

Sterling Publications

2291 Avent Ferry Road, Suite 215

Raleigh, NC 27606

1-888-476-6268 (toll-free)

romantc@aol.com

*A one-year subscription (six issues) is $15; two years, $25.*


STEPFAMILIES

Clergy Services

706 W. 42nd St.

Kansas City, MO 64111

1-800-237-1922 (toll-free)

*This group offers family medallions and ceremonies to incorporate children in weddings.*


The Stepfamily Association of America, Inc.

650 J St., Suite 205

Lincoln, NE 68508

(402) 477-STEP

*This group offers a newsletter and books for parents, teens, and kids.*

# ACKNOWLEDGMENTS

Thanks to these people who shared their experience and wisdom: Bob and Nikki Cassidy, Cheryl and Greg Conrad, Patty Duke, Cliff and Regina Ellis, DeLoss "Dee" Friesen, Shawn Julian, Pete and Donna Kaufman, Leslie Lafayette, Mary Lansing, Ralph and Irene Lindholm, Stephanie McCaleb, Yolanda and Brian McVicker, Don and Melaney Moisan, Dick and Patty Montgomery, Ray and Wanda Morris, Kelly and Chris Swinford, Kate and Doug Verigin, Michael and Athena Webb, David Worthington—and those who shared their stories anonymously.

Thanks also to editor Sandy Rowe, for her consent to using material originally published in *The Sunday Oregonian*, and to computer whiz Richard Edinger, for his patience and expertise.

# OTHER BOOKS FROM
# BEYOND WORDS PUBLISHING, INC.

## ADULTS'

### HOME SWEETER HOME:
### CREATING A HAVEN OF SIMPLICITY AND SPIRIT
*Author: Jann Mitchell; Foreword: Jack Canfield, $12.95 softcover*

We search the world for spirituality and peace—only to discover that happiness and satisfaction are not found "out there" in the world but right here in our houses and in our hearts. Award-winning journalist and author Jann Mitchell offers creative insights and suggestions for making our home life more nurturing, spiritual, and rewarding for ourselves, our families, and our friends.

### THE WOMAN'S BOOK OF CREATIVITY
*Author: C Diane Ealy, $12.95 softcover*

Creativity works differently in women and men, and women are most creative when they tap into the process that is unique to their own nature—a holistic, "spiraling" approach. The book is a self-help manual, both inspirational and practical, for igniting female creative fire. Ealy encourages women to acknowledge their own creativity, often in achievements they take for granted. She also gives a wealth of suggestions and exercises to enable women to recognize their own creative power and to access it consistently and effectively. Ealy holds a doctorate in behavioral science and consults with individuals and corporations on creativity.

## NURTURING SPIRITUALITY IN CHILDREN
*Author: Peggy D. Jenkins, $10.95 softcover*

Children who develop a healthy balance of mind and spirit enter adulthood with higher self-esteem, better able to respond to life's challenges. This book offers scores of simple and thought-provoking lessons that parents can teach to their children in less than ten minutes at a time. Using items easily found around the house, each lesson provides a valuable message for children to take into their days and into their lives. The lessons are easy to prepare and understand, and each parent can alter the lessons to fit their own spiritual beliefs. The activities are adaptable for children from preschool to high school ages.

## THE BOOK OF GODDESSES
*Author/illustrator: Kris Waldherr*
*Introduction: Linda Schierse Leonard, Ph.D., $17.95 hardcover*

This beautifully illustrated book introduces readers of all ages to twenty-six goddesses and heroines from cultures around the world. In the descriptions of these archetypal women, the author weaves a picture of the beauty, individuality, and unique strength which are the birthright of every girl and woman. Beautiful to look at and inspiring to read, this book is a stunning gift for goddess-lovers of all ages.

## KNOW YOUR TRUTH. SPEAK YOUR TRUTH. LIVE YOUR TRUTH
*Author: Eileen R. Hannegan, $12.95 softcover*

To be truly yourself, you need to have an authentic integration of the mental, emotional, physical, and spiritual truths of self. This book offers a simplified formula of the ancient truths that escort an individual into personal and spiritual wholeness. The three-part program assists individuals in discovering the truth of who they truly are and thereby in living a more authentic life.

## YOU CAN HAVE IT ALL
*Author: Arnold M. Patent, $16.95 hardcover*

Joy, peace, abundance—these gifts of the Universe are available to each of us whenever we choose to play the real game of life: the game of mutual support. *You Can Have It All* is a guidebook that shows us how to move beyond our beliefs in struggle and shortage, open our hearts, and enjoy a life of true ecstasy. Arnold Patent first self-published *You Can Have It All* in 1984, and it became a classic with over 200,000 copies in print. This revised and expanded edition reflects his greater understanding of the principles and offers practical suggestions as well as simple exercises for improving the quality of our lives.

## LETTERS FROM THE LIGHT:
## AN AFTERLIFE JOURNAL FROM THE SELF-LIGHTED WORLD
*Author: Elsa Barker; Editor: Kathy Hart, $18.95 hardcover*

In the early part of this century, a woman begins a process of "automatic writing." It is as though someone takes over her hand and writes the document. Days later she finds out that the man has died thousands of miles away, and she is now serving as a conduit as he tells of life after death through her. His message: There is nothing to fear in death, and the life after this one is similar in many ways to the one we already know, even though we will be much more able to recognize our freedom.

Readers of the book, originally published in 1914, invariably concur that the book removed from them the fear of dying.

## RITES OF PASSAGE:
## CELEBRATING LIFE'S CHANGES
*Authors: Kathleen Wall, Ph.D., and Gary Ferguson, $12.95 softcover*

Every major transition in our lives—be it marriage, high-school graduation, the death of a parent or spouse, or the last child leaving home—brings with it opportunities for growth and self-actualization, for repositioning ourselves in the world. Personal ritual—the focus of *Rites of Passage*—allows us to use the energy held within the anxiety of change to nourish the new person that is forever struggling to be born. *Rites of Passage* begins by explaining to readers that human growth is not linear, as many of us assume, but rather occurs in a four-part cycle. After sharing the patterns of transition, the authors then show the reader how ritual can help him or her move through these specific life changes: work and career, intimate relationships, friends, divorce, changes within the family, adolescence, issues in the last half of life, and personal loss.

## QUESTIONS FOR MY FATHER:
## FINDING THE MAN BEHIND YOUR DAD
*Author: Vin Staniforth, $15.00 hardcover*

*Questions for My Father* is a little book that asks big questions—some serious, some playful, some risky. Each question is an opportunity to open, rejuvenate, or bring closure to the powerful but often overlooked relationship between fathers and children. Fathers have long been regarded as objects of mystery and fascination. *Questions for My Father* provides a blueprint for uncovering the full dimensions of the man behind the mystery. It offers a way to let fathers tell their personal stories and to let children explore their own knowledge and understanding of one of the largest figures in their lives. In rediscovering their dad, readers will discover themselves.

## A Guy's Guide to Pregnancy
*Author: Frank Mungeam; Foreword: John Gray, $12.95 softcover*

Every day, 4,000 American men become first-time dads. There are literally hundreds of pregnancy guides aimed at women, but guys rarely rate more than a footnote. What men need is *A Guy's Guide to Pregnancy*, the first book to explain, in guy terms, the changes that happen to his partner and their relationship during pregnancy. *A Guy's Guide to Pregnancy* is written by and for men with a humorous yet insightful approach. The book is organized to be approachable in appearance as well as content and is divided into forty brisk chapters, one for each week of the pregnancy. The length of the book is intentionally shorter than the epic texts aimed at women. The result is a book about pregnancy that men will actually read because it presents pregnancy from a man's point of view.

## The Complete Guide to Wheat-Free Cooking
*Author: Phyllis Potts, $14.95 softcover*

More than a collection of delicious recipes, *The Complete Guide to Wheat-Free Cooking* celebrates the joys of eating well and encourages the reader to seek foods that maximize health and vitality. Potts chose treasured family recipes—good old-fashioned comfort food—and modified them for people like herself who can't eat wheat. As an insider, she has invaluable insights into what it takes to succeed at making a dramatic diet change. She shows readers how to reproduce the textures and flavors of breads and pastries using non-wheat flours made from rice, garbonzo beans, and corn. She also teaches creativity in working with substitutions for those with multiple food allergies. The book includes recipes for just about everything: breads, soups, main courses, sauces, even desserts and candy. All the recipes are easy to follow and economical to prepare. Potts wants the reader to enjoy making these recipes and gives many helpful hints for doing it right the first time.

## CREATE YOUR OWN LOVE STORY: THE ART OF LASTING RELATIONSHIPS

*Author: David W. McMillan, Ph.D.*

*Foreword: John Gray, $21.95 hardcover; $14.95 softcover*

Create Your Own Love Story breaks new ground in the crowded and popular field of relationship self-help guides. *Create Your Own Love Story* is based on a four-part model—Spirit, Trust, Trade, and Art—derived from McMillan's twenty years' work in community theory and clinical psychology. Each of these four elements is divided into short, highly readable chapters that include both touching and hilarious examples from real marriages, brief exercises based on visualization and journal writing that are effective whether used by one or both partners, and dialogues that readers can have with themselves and/or their partners. This book shows readers how they can use their own energy and initiative, with McMillan's help, to make their marriages stronger, more enduring, and more soul-satisfying.

## The Intuitive Way:
## A Guide to Living from Inner Wisdom
*Author: Penney Peirce; Foreword: Carol Adrienne, $16.95 softcover*

When intuition is in full bloom, life takes on a magical, effortless quality; your world is suddenly full of synchronicities, creative insights, and abundant knowledge just for the asking. *The Intuitive Way* shows you how to enter that state of perceptual aliveness and integrate it into daily life to achieve greater natural flow through an easy-to-understand, ten-step course. Author Penney Peirce synthesizes teachings from psychology, East-West philosophy, religion, metaphysics, and business. In simple and direct language, Peirce describes the intuitive process as a new way of life and demonstrates many practical applications from speeding decision-making to expanding personal growth. Whether you're just beginning to search for a richer, fuller life experience or are looking for more subtle, sophisticated insights about your spiritual path, *The Intuitive Way* will be your companion as you progress through the stages of intuition development.

## Embracing the Goddess Within
*Author/illustrator: Kris Waldherr, $17.95 hardcover*

*Embracing the Goddess Within* is the companion to the author's best-selling *Book of Goddesses*. Based upon her extensive research of cultures and traditions around the world, Waldherr presents evocative illustrations and simple but powerful stories and rituals to help guide women through the rites of passage that mark their lives. *Embracing the Goddess Within* alternates beautiful illustrations with gold-and-sepia-bordered text that conveys the mystique and wisdom of each particular goddess, along with rituals for accessing her power. It takes the goddess trend to the next level by combining a resourceful self-help approach with a stunning visual presentation. It's fun, feminine, and sexy—and will make a beautiful gift that appeals to women of all ages.

## LETTERS TO OUR DAUGHTERS:
## MOTHERS' WORDS OF LOVE
*Authors: Kristine Van Raden and Molly Davis, $19.95 hardcover*

*Letters to Our Daughters* brings together letters from mothers to their daughters from around the world and from all walks of life. What unites these writings is that regardless of life circumstances, education, beliefs, economic status, or age, each mother rejoices in the uniqueness of her daughter and desires for her a future filled with hope, strength, and self-worth. The book includes over forty letters and photos of mothers and daughters who share their stories of courage and triumph, pain and loss, wisdom and love. Touching and inspirational, *Letters to Our Daughters* makes a perfect gift for all women. It can become a cherished keepsake because it provides a place in which the reader can place her own personal letter and photograph. The authors have written an invitation to the reader in which they suggest ways each individual mother can compose her own unique message of love.

## SACRED FLOWERS:
## CREATING A HEAVENLY GARDEN
*Author: Roni Jay, $14.95 hardcover*

How can a bouquet of daffodils, the scent of a rose, or the quiet contemplation of a solitary lily on an altar move someone to ineffable joy, uplift a trodden spirit, or instill a profound sense of calm and well-being? As author Roni Jay reveals in this exquisitely crafted little book, many common flowering plants—including the daisy, the violet, and the morning glory—have been held sacred by religions and cultures throughout the ages, not only as divine symbols but also for their unique healing and enhancing powers for the body, mind, and spirit. With lyric prose and richly hued botanical illustrations, the author guides us to many of these sacred flowers found—or easily grown—in one's window box or garden. *Sacred Flowers* is a delightful reference and a practical guide to discovering special gifts and magical powers on a journey to personal enlightenment.

## CHILDREN'S

### FROG GIRL

*Author: Paul Owen Lewis, $14.95 hardcover*

This stunning follow-up to the critically acclaimed, best-selling *Storm Boy* tells the story of an American Indian girl who discovers that the frogs around her village have disappeared. Journeying to the mysterious underwater realm of the Frog People, she receives an ominous message from Volcano Woman: to save her village from the destruction she must solve the mystery of the vanishing frogs. Full of bravery and adventure, this story will inspire young girls to trust in their abilities. During a time in which the earth's ecosystems are sending us dire warnings through the true disappearance of many species of frogs, *Frog Girl* reminds us that it is time to take responsibility for the earth and to respect the creatures we share it with.

## GIRLS KNOW BEST
*Editor: Michelle Roehm, $8.95 softcover*

*Girls Know Best* contains the writings of thirty-eight different girls from across the United States. The book is divided into chapters focusing on specific issues and giving advice from the girl writers to the girl readers. The topics include living with siblings, school/homework, parents, divorce and dealing with stepfamilies, boys, friends, losses when your best friend moves away or you do, depression, dealing with differences (race and religion), drugs, our bodies and looks, and overcoming life's biggest obstacles. Each writing includes a photo of the girl author and a brief background about her and her dreams. Breaking up these chapters are fun activities that girls can do together or by themselves, including best-friend crafts, ways kids can save the environment, ideas for volunteering, natural beauty fun, and even how to pass notes in class without getting caught. The book is a vehicle for encouraging girls to use their creativity and to believe in themselves and their infinite potential. By showing that any girl can do it, our girl authors will be models and inspirations for all girls.

## GIRLS WHO ROCKED THE WORLD:
## HEROINES FROM SACAGAWEA TO SHERYL SWOOPES
*Author: Amelie Welden, $8.95 softcover*

*Girls Who Rocked the World* is the follow-up to *Girls Know Best*. Both books encourage girls to believe in themselves and go for their dreams.

*Girls Who Rocked the World* tells the stories of thirty-five real girls, past and present, from all around the world, who achieved amazing feats and changed history *before reaching their twenties*. Included are well-known girls like Helen Keller and Sacagawea as well as many often-overlooked heroines such as Joan of Arc, Phillis Wheatley, and Wang Yani. Interspersed along with the stories of heroines are photos and writings of real girls from all over America answering the question, "How do I plan to rock the world?" By highlighting the goals and dreams of these girls, the book links these historical heroines to girls today who will be the next ones to rock the world!

## THE BOOK OF FAIRIES:
### NATURE SPIRITS FROM AROUND THE WORLD
*Author: Rose Williams; Illustrator: Robin T. Barrett, $18.95 hardcover*

This exquisite anthology of tales from the fairy realms brings together stories from all over the world. Fairies are part of the oral tradition of many cultures, and the stories about them often reveal them in a healing capacity, teaching human beings the secrets of nature and showing them how to live more peacefully and harmoniously. The stories in this collection are enchanting in every way—they sparkle with magic, adventure, and romance as well as revealing the connections between fairies and the natural world. In these pages, you can walk with Connla and Nora on clouds of gold, amber, purple, and red in "The Golden Spear," from Ireland; visit the mermaids, the pixies, and the fire-gnomes in the English tale "The Fairies' Jewels"; and sing and dance by the moonlit riverbank with Soma and Surya in "The Mountains of the Moon," from the Indian tradition. *The Book of Fairies* will introduce you to all kinds of good and evil characters from both the spirit and the human worlds. With its timeless themes and delicately crafted illustrations, this is an anthology to be treasured for life.

To order or to request a catalog, contact
BEYOND WORDS PUBLISHING, INC.
20827 N.W. Cornell Road, Suite 500
Hillsboro, OR 97124-9808
503-531-8700 or 1-800-284-9673

# Beyond Words Publishing, Inc.

Our corporate mission:

Inspire to Integrity

Our declared values:

We give to all of life as life has given us.
We honor all relationships.
Trust and stewardship are integral to fulfilling dreams.
Collaboration is essential to create miracles.
Creativity and aesthetics nourish the soul.
Unlimited thinking is fundamental.
Living your passion is vital.
Joy and humor open our hearts to growth.
It is important to remind ourselves of love.